COURT SENSE

COURT SENSE
The Invisible Edge in Basketball and Life

by George A. Selleck, Ph.D.

Foreword by Richard Lapchick, Ph.D.

Diamond Communications, Inc.
South Bend, Indiana

COURT SENSE
The Invisible Edge in Basketball and Life

10 9 8 7 6 5 4 3 2 1

Manufactured in the United States of America

Diamond Communications, Inc.
Post Office Box 88
South Bend, Indiana 46624-0088
Editorial: (219) 299-9278
Orders Only: 1-800-480-3717
Fax: (219) 299-9296
Website: www.diamondbooks.com

Library of Congress Cataloging-in-Publication Data
Selleck, George A. (George Abraham), 1934 -
    Court sense : the invisible edge in basketball and life / by
George A. Selleck ; foreword by Richard Lapchick.
        p.   cm.
    ISBN 1-888698-16-0
    1. Basketball--Psychological aspects. 2. Sports--
Psychological aspects. 3. Athletes--Life skills guides. 4.
Success. I. Title.
GV889.2.S45   1999
798.323'01--dc21   98-30983
                                                              CIP

CONTENTS

PART THREE
HOW DO YOU COACH COURT SENSE?

FOREWORD

In the 1998 Western Conference Finals, the Los Angeles Lakers were favored to beat the Utah Jazz, even though the Jazz owned the best record in the NBA. After all, the Lakers were young, talented, and had four All-Stars on their squad. The Jazz were old, boring, and dressed funny. Nevertheless, in four methodical games, the Jazz literally swept the Lakers under the carpet. Jazz coach Jerry Sloan had said when the series started that the team that played with the most intelligence had the best chance of winning.

Never underestimate the power of an athlete who knows how to think.

Today, being a successful athlete is not just about technical proficiency—the jump shot, the curveball, the perfect dig. Today's athletes need to be able to think critically and play well—at the same time. They need to have Court Sense.

Court sense isn't a primer for showing athletes how to stand at the free throw line or what plays to run when the score is tied and there are five seconds left on the clock. Instead, it tells athletes how to "play smart." Athletes with court sense know how to read teammates, assess opponents' weaknesses, and know how and when to utilize their own strengths—when to steal second, when to take the shot or dish-off to a teammate, when to spike the ball.

These thinking skills don't just apply to sports, however. The skills that athletes need to think on their feet during a game are the same skills they need to figure out a geometry problem, decide on a career, or work through a relationship. Thus, the second—and most important—thing court sense does is to show athletes how to transfer the thinking skills they learn on the athletic field to everyday situations in their lives. To do this, Dr. Selleck uses experiences from his own career as a Hall-of-Fame basketball player, coach, referee, psychologist and educator—along with stories and examples taken straight from today's sports headlines.

It is Dr. Selleck's belief that every skill necessary for a productive and successful life can be learned from sports, and that participation can help young people—regardless of the depth of their sports experience—develop concrete life skills that will prepare them to become successful adults and community leaders.

Court sense should be of vital interest to athletes, coaches, educators, and leaders in the sports community. No matter what sport is involved, the lessons contained in court sense are viable tools to help teach students of all ages critical thinking skills. As a sociologist and educator, what I like most is the universal applicability of its lessons and the fact that court sense is appropriate for athletes of any skill level.

Because 40 million youth participate in sports programs every year, sport becomes a universal language that everyone can relate to in some way—whether as a player, supporter, or viewer. As Dr. Selleck points out, sport is fun, interactive, and emotional. This makes it a powerful context for learning and the ideal vehicle to convey important messages to a captive audience. Whenever we can make sport and its athletes better, we move toward creating a better society. With the addition of court sense, we are succeeding in doing just that.

Richard Lapchick, Ph.D.
Center Director
The Center for the Study of Sport in Society

ABOUT THE AUTHOR

My first personal recollection of George Selleck occurred in the spring of 1953 when I was pitching batting practice for the Stanford freshman team. As a transfer student from Colgate University and, therefore, ineligible for a year, I was working out with the frosh. After throwing a number of pitches high, wide, and hardly handsome, Selleck yelled out to me, "Come on, give me something to hit."

I thought, "Oh, great," I was going to have to put up with a prima donna. I mean, after all, at 5'8" and 140 pounds, George was not exactly an easy target to pitch to. And his reputation as an exceptional athlete from glitzy Southern California preceded him. He had been "all everything" at Compton High School including the state's high school basketball "Player of the Year" when he led his team to a 32-0 record. His initial exploit at Stanford was pacing the freshman Cagers—alongside his to-be backcourt mate, Ron Wagner—to a gaudy 18-1 mark. So in consecutive years, Selleck basketball teams had been 50-1!

Well, my initial diamond take on George was certainly in error. He wasn't being arrogant or getting on my case, he was just exhibiting one of his enduring traits—that of wanting to get as much out of practice time as possible. I came to realize that George was never satisfied with anything but the best, either from his team or himself. He was extremely critical of himself and worked harder than anyone on the squad, both in games—whatever the game—and at practice.

I really got to know George after the Stanford baseball coaches decided I wrote a better game than I played. As a result, I spent my Stanford career partly as sports editor of the student newspaper, *The Stanford Daily*, and also covering Stanford sports for local newspapers in Palo Alto and San Jose.

I owe George a lot! He was great copy—on and off the court. He led by example and was the epitome of this book, *Court Sense*. To do the things he did, he had to play smart. Phil Woolpert, who guided USF to basketball greatness with Bill Russell and K.C. Jones, referred to George as "the Bob Cousy of the West." I had the good fortune of growing up in the East and saw Cousy—the Holy Cross All-American—perform several times at Madison Square Garden. Cousy was a magician on the court. Woolpert was certainly right on target in his comparison. And for latter-day readers, perhaps we could refer to John Stockton as "the George Selleck of this era."

In my senior year, George led the unsung Stanford cagers to a 17-8 record and a second-place finish in the then-Pac-8 Southern Division. The following season, he was named an All-American. He spurned an opportunity to play professional basketball, preferring to expand his horizons, pursuing graduate work at Stanford, Princeton, and the University of Southern California, earning a doctorate in counseling.

Always striving for excellence, George has worn many hats during the tenure of his career. Building on his love of sport, George served as a basketball coach at Brentwood High School where he was twice named "High School Coach of the Year" by the *Los Angeles Times*. He then went on to serve as an NCAA referee for 15 years. Integrating his training in psychology with his athletic experience, George has shared his knowledge with sporting outfits on every level—from elementary school to professional teams—including the NBA Rookie Transition Program, American Basketball Coaches' Association, U.S. Tennis Association, the annual Volleyball Festival for Women, and the coaching staffs of more than 90-member NCAA institutions.

In the mid-1990s, George began to focus on the untapped educational potential of sports and the tremendous impact it could have on youth. He began to develop programs and materials that would greatly enhance the youth sports experience and bridge the gap between sports and education. In 1995, George wrote *How to Play the Game of Your Life: A Guide to Success in Sports and Life*, and argued that sports can effectively prepare kids for life, by helping them to develop important life success skills. In 1997 he founded Sports for Life—a nonprofit organization exclusively dedicated to this mission—to maximize the educational value of sports and to enhance youth development through positive participation in sports and physical activity. At publication time, Sports for Life—under George's direction—has reached out to more than 10,000 students and adults—promoting the valuable relationship between sports and education. George's lifelong dedication was highlighted by his selection to receive the 1997 Distinguished Service Award

About the Author

from the California State Athletic Directors Association (CSADA) for his service to interscholastic athletics—a commitment that remains unfaltering.

As I refreshed my memory for this brief review of the life and good times of George Selleck, I was struck by the similarities between the rules he lived and played by during his Stanford years and the rules young men and women athletes and their coaches so urgently need today in what is a far different environment. George was a prolific scorer at Stanford—third on the all-time list at the time of this graduation and still on the top twenty list today; but perhaps more impressive was his court management style in which he made his teammates better players.

In *Court Sense* George passes along unerring advice about how to think on your feet and transfer sports skills to other areas of life. *Court Sense* holds that sports can be used as a tool to teach kids how to develop critical thinking skills and attempts to help the athletic community make a solid contribution to youth education. In demonstrating the positive connection between playing smart on the court and making wise life choices, the "Selleck experience" is an unquestionably fertile training ground.

As I wind up this George Selleck "look back" and "look ahead" piece, I still wonder about one aspect of his development as an athlete: "George, didn't any of my pitches come across the plate?"

Russ Wilks
Stanford Sports Scribe, 1952-55

IN MEMORY OF

George Kellogg, 1892 - 1982 (YMCA Coach)

Ken Fagans, 1909 - 1994 (High School Coach)

Howie Dallmar, 1922 - 1991 (College Coach)

ACKNOWLEDGMENTS

I would like to acknowlege, with gratitude, teammates and coaches whose love for the game of basketball and willingness to share themselves on the court, have each in their own way contributed to this work. Particular thanks to...

...*My teammates at Compton High School:* Harold Graham, Delbert Johnston, Deward Mitchell, George Pierson, Woody Sauldsberry, Bob Savage, and Al Waner

...*My teammates at Stanford University:* Carlos Bea, Bill Bond, Barry Brown, Don DeLong, Dave Dunn, Beppo Dyer, Dave Epperson, Bill Flanders, Gary Van Galder, Carl Issacs, Jim Johnson, Russ Lawler, Bob McGrath, Leo Schwaiger, Oleg Suzdaleff, Ron Tomsic, Bill Turner, Hap Wagner, and Ron Wagner

...*My junior, senior high, and college coaches:* Ed Moore, Ken Fagans, and Howie Dallmar

I wish to acknowledge my present teammates, the Board of Directors of *Sports for Life, Inc. Sports for Life* was founded as a nonprofit organization in 1997 to promote the value of sports education—preparing children to become successful adults and community leaders through involvement in the sports experience. Through specialized leadership training, curricula, and workshop development, *Sports for Life* works to create community and school-based programs nationwide. Thank you for your ongoing support in conveying the vital message of sports education and for continuing to play a significant role in the success of *Sports for Life*—Bill Barnes, Frank Boren, Dave Epperson, David Goad, Allan Goodman, Paul McDonald, Brad Muster, John Prichard, Howie Rubin, Tom Waterhouse, Rick Wolff, and Naomi Goldman, our director of development—you are all winners in the biggest game of all—life!

Special thanks to Dave Bollwinkel, Arthur Costa, Mike Montgomery, Pete Newell, Robert Sternberg, and John Wooden for their time and thoughts in discussing this project with me, and Brad Leonard for his critiques and contributions to the manuscript.

Lastly, a most significant thank you to Wendy Fayles, who helped me throughout this process of transforming ideas and experiences into a book. Her understanding of my interests and commitments, and her outstanding skills were essential to this project.

INTRODUCTION

Basketball is not for stupid people.
> - Tara VanDerveer, Olympic and college basketball coach

In the fall of 1996, Jill Langford—the publisher of my book, *How to Play the Game of Your Life*—called to ask me if I'd be willing to write another book called *The Mental Game of Basketball*. She already had two very successful books in her stable along those lines (*The Mental Game of Baseball* and *The Mental Game of Golf*) and figured with my basketball background I'd be a good choice to write the third.

It took me all of two seconds to say, "No."

My reasoning was that it sounded like another sports psychology book, and I'm really not into that kind of stuff. Besides, I was already quite busy with my work in helping athletes learn how to transfer sports skills to life skills. But over the next few months some things happened that caused me to change my mind.

DARWIN'S ATHLETES

First, I read a book by John Hoberman, a sports historian at the University of Texas-Austin, called *Darwin's Athletes*. In his book, Hoberman makes the point that black inner-city youth are being misled into thinking that the best way for them to get ahead is to be successful at sports. Hoberman goes on to note that in our technologically driven world, it is intellectual skills—not physical skills—that these young people need to focus on in order to succeed.

Various other people have expressed concerns about the role sports play in the lives of young athletes—especially young black athletes. According to a 1991 study by sociologist Jay Coakley, only one young black male in 153,000 will make it to the NBA. Harry Edwards of the University of California says that the single-minded effort by young athletes causes them to ignore other talents, leaving them short-changed when their sports careers don't pan out.

Even for those athletes who do achieve the goal of playing professionally, their careers are often short and don't guarantee that they will never have to work again. In the case of female professional basketball players, for example, where salaries are nowhere near the level of male players, some women barely make enough to support themselves *during* their careers—let alone after!

Anyway, after reading Hoberman's book I immediately thought of the millions of kids playing basketball who love the game and dream of playing in the pros some day. What do we tell them? Don't play? Concentrate on your schoolwork instead? Give up your dreams?

Realistically speaking, Hoberman is right. In a world that is driven by technology and brainpower, it is our ability to think that will ensure a successful life. *But what if*, I thought, *what if basketball could be used as a tool to teach kids how to think?* Couldn't they then transfer that skill to the rest of their lives? They could have the dream, but if it didn't work out, they wouldn't be left empty-handed.

The question that any young person faces is this: What are the possibilities in my life? A young person in the inner city is less likely to be exposed to the corporate world or even the educational world. What they are likely to be exposed to is the athletic world. Thus, it is our responsibility to make sure that *that* world introduces athletes to and equips them for the possibilities that lie outside the world of sport.

I THOUGHT OF ALL THE TIMES I POINTED TO MY HEAD AND SAID, "THINK!"

Second, I remembered all the times spent coaching youth and high school basketball when I would point to my head and say, "Think!" What did I mean by that? What did I want my players to think about? How did I want them to think?

Most importantly, why was such thinking necessary? After all, I have talked to many basketball coaches about this subject and most of them say they don't want their players thinking while they're playing. They are convinced that if the coaches do the thinking and the players do the playing, the game will flow automatically.

On the other hand, coaches do want their players to play intelligently. To me, that naturally raises the question: How can you play intelligently without thinking?

Well, you can't. And if you look closely at the best athletes in the game—the athletes whom I would call "complete" players—you will see that one of the things that they have in common is their ability to think and play at the same time. I call this ability **court sense**.

COURT SENSE: AN ESSENTIAL INGREDIENT FOR A COMPLETE PLAYER

To be a complete player requires a combination of four things:

(1) **Athleticism**. This means you have to have excellent physical skills. Of all the things it takes to be a complete player, this is the area over which you have the least control. After all, if you were born to be 5'8," there's nothing you can do to make yourself taller. You do, however, have control over whether you keep your physical self in top condition, regardless of what natural abilities you may have been given. Exercising that control is part of court sense.

(2) **Fundamentals**. This means being able to execute the basic skills of the game—passing, dribbling, shooting, defense, etc. You can have excellent physical skills, but still be lousy at the fundamentals (just ask any 7-footer who excelled in high school basketball but struggled in college or the pros.) Knowing the fundamentals can make someone with average physical skills a great player—and it can make someone with excellent physical skills a complete player. Consider Debbie Black. At 5'3" tall, she's the shortest player in the American Basketball League. She's also the one with the longest contract—because her outstanding fundamentals makes her one of the strongest defensive players in the league. Recognizing the importance of fundamentals and being willing to work hard to master them is part of court sense.

(3) **Character**. What is your attitude toward others? Toward life? Do you treat people with respect? Do you keep agreements? Do you

know how to exercise self-control? Do you hold yourself to a higher standard of behavior? Athletes with court sense understand that their character, or the kind of person they are, helps determine their success on and off the court.

(4) **Court sense**. Simply put, court sense means using your head to improve your playing ability. It includes the things we've already talked about, plus:

- A thorough knowledge of basketball—everything from knowing the rules of the game to knowing how the way different gymnasiums are set up can affect your play

- The ability to develop game-winning strategies that make the most of your strengths

- The ability to anticipate what others are going to do, and make appropriate adjustments

- How you think about the game on and off the court

The point is, if your goal is to become a really good basketball player, natural ability is not enough. No matter what game you play—basketball, volleyball, football, softball, tennis, or golf—developing your "court sense" will help you take your game to a higher level.

THERE IS MORE TO BASKETBALL THAN THE SLAM-DUNK OR THE LONG TREY

Court awareness as part of basketball intelligence has gone out the window.

> - Dave Bollwinkel, college basketball coach

Coaches are constantly complaining that players these days just don't understand the game. Why is that, they ask?

Here's one answer. In *The Mental Game of Baseball*, the authors

Introduction

note that coaches spend little time teaching mental skills and strategies. Coaches tend to explain this by saying that they are expert only in the physical elements of the game. The players are left on their own when it comes to developing their mental skills. Often when athletes focus exclusively on their physical skills, they are forced to learn their mental lessons the hard way, or not at all.

But it's not just the coaches. Too many athletes also underestimate the importance of court sense. The Los Angeles Lakers, for example, were dumbfounded when the old (and supposedly decrepit) Utah Jazz swept them in the 1998 Western Conference Finals. The Lakers should have taken a clue from the previous year's playoff experience. For example, in an article in *The Orange County Register*, sportswriter Steve Bisheff described the bad game the Los Angeles Lakers had against the Utah Jazz in Game 2 of the Western Conference semifinals in 1997. With just over two seconds remaining and the game tied, the Lakers made the mistake of fouling Jazzman Antoine Carr. Carr promptly sank two free throws and the Jazz went on to win the game and the series.

As Bisheff noted, the Lakers fouled the wrong player. If they had fouled John Stockton in the lane before Carr had a chance to shoot, the game probably would have gone into overtime. It also would have helped if the Lakers had avoided the five technicals they received for playing illegal defenses—not to mention the technical slapped on Nick Van Exel for swearing at a referee. Add all those "free" points together, and the outcome of the game would have been much different. Laker Eddie Jones tried to explain the problem by saying, "We've got so much talent, we tend not to use our heads. We have so much athleticism, we think we can get by on that. They're [the Jazz] just the opposite. They are a smart, heady team. A team that doesn't get distracted. Maybe because they don't have as much raw talent, they have to use their heads."

Unfortunately, playing smart has given way to the flying dunk and the long three-point shot. The value of knowing how to play in different basketball situations has been minimized in the minds of players and coaches.

No wonder there appears to be a major disconnection between

sports and intelligence. People just don't see how the two are connected. However, as my friend Bill Barnes says, "All athletic endeavor is an intellectual activity." In other words, how can you successfully perform unless you have an understanding of the game? Athletic skills have a built-in-limit. When I played basketball at Stanford University, there were a whole lot of guys who were quicker than I (especially after my fifth knee operation), and since I never exceeded 5'8" in height, almost all of them where taller. Yet I was able to outplay all of them some of the time and some of them all of the time because I could out-think them. Court sense gave me that edge.

COURT SENSE—THE NEXT LEVEL OF EXCELLENCE

In the world of basketball, much has been done to help players approach their physical limits. Thousands of books have been written, hundreds of camps have been held —all with the goal of helping athletes develop the proper form and technique.

To give athletes a mental edge, sports psychology has examined the process of how the mind can influence athletic performance. By teaching athletes how to focus, visualize, and so on, sports psychology gets them in the right mind-set for most games.

All this is helpful to improving athletic performance. However, among top athletes these factors usually balance out. So where do we go next? To court sense: the understanding of the game that seems to be lacking in so many of today's players.

SO WHY AM I WRITING THIS BOOK?

We learn by doing, if we reflect on what we have done.
- John Dewey

All of this brings me back to why I decided to write this book after all. First, I believe recognizing the value of court sense can help young athletes play the game better, and can help coaches coach the game better. After all, I love basketball, and I remember vividly what it is

Introduction

like to be young and to have dreams, and to want to see those dreams come true.

Make no mistakes, though. This book is not about what plays to run or drills to use. It's not about how to shoot better or jump higher. This book is about court savvy or awareness. It is about the kind of thinking any athlete must do to perform at his or her best.

Secondly, I believe that by helping athletes develop their court sense, we can stimulate their interest in the process of learning. Sports are such a great and largely unrecognized tool for helping kids learn! One reason sports can be so successful as a teaching tool is because they offer the three most critical components of learning: Sports are:

- **Emotional**. When you play sports, you connect to what you are doing. People learn best when they feel a connection to what they are learning.

- **Interactive**. Hands-on learning is easier to remember. There is also considerable evidence that children can learn much better in well-configured cooperative groupings than they can on their own.

- **Fun!** When you're having fun, it's not likely that your mind is wandering to other things.

Intelligence, like sports, is a lot about confidence. I never had much respect for my own intelligence, and nobody else did either (or if they did, they never told me about it). I was always "the basketball player." It was an easy way to identify me, and it was easy for me to buy into. Athletes don't get a lot of support for their thinking ability. Many basketball coaches have taught their players *not* to think. But if you take thinking out of a player's game, it reduces the player to the status of a robot.

Finally, I believe that a player's court sense can lead to the development of the kind of thinking skills that are essential to achieving success *off* the court. If you can use basketball to learn better thinking skills, then that knowledge can be transferred to the classroom, your personal relationships, your decision making, your career, and so on.

For everyone who is not destined to become a millionaire pro athlete (and even for those few who are) there is a need to think intelligently in order to have a decent standard of living in the 21st century.

There is also a need to be able to think intelligently when life doesn't work out the way you planned it. Because it's a plain fact that things go wrong. Mistakes happen. Accidents happen. They happen in basketball all the time. You think your team is a shoo-in for the NBA Finals and three of your top players get benched during the play-offs. Or you play a team for the league championship that you beat decisively earlier in the season, and they pull an upset.

After Dan O'Brien failed to make the U.S. Olympic team in 1992 (when he was favored to win the gold medal in the decathlon), he commented: "I grew as a person after that. I realized that no matter how hard you've trained or how hard you've practiced, something can go wrong. Nothing is for sure. I had to readjust my goals and my thinking." The ability to make the adjustments necessary to improve his game led O'Brien to Olympic gold four years later—and underscored the fact that even the best athletes can do better with court sense.

Court sense helps you become more adaptable to changes during the game. When things aren't going the way you planned, you must be able to work with what you have. For example, several years ago there was a large fire in the Interstate Bank building in Los Angeles. Two investment managers were working late at night several floors above where the fire started. When they smelled smoke, they tried the phones, which were dead. The elevator was not working. There was smoke in the stairwell. When they tried to break the office windows, the glass was too strong. What could they do to avoid dying from smoke inhalation?

They opened file cabinets to breathe from the air that was in them. They moistened paper towels and used them as filters to claim the air from the empty water cooler jugs. They used their heads in a situation they'd never dreamed of or planned for, and they survived. They had court sense.

When kids learn how to "learn" the game of basketball, they are also learning how to "learn" for the game of life. Think about it.

Introduction

What is basketball? It's a problem to be solved. The athlete "solves" the problem by using a combination of court sense and fundamental basketball skills that have been practiced and prepared until they are automatic.

What is life? It's a series of problems to be solved. With the right conditioning, athletes can learn how to transfer the same learning process that provides them with court sense to life off the court. Remember the old saying? "Give a man a fish, and you feed him for a day; teach a man to fish and you feed him for a lifetime"? When you teach a basketball player how to play, you're in essence "feeding him for a day." But when you teach that athlete how to think, you're feeding him for a lifetime.

PART ONE

WHAT IS COURT SENSE?

Chapter  1

WHAT COURT SENSE IS...
AND ISN'T

It's years and years of constant training and practice. I didn't do anything differently last season. It's just that all of a sudden your mental skills, and your physical skills and your knowledge of the game come together.
- Brady Anderson, Baltimore Orioles center fielder

He can't move, he can only do a couple of things, so he has to play smart.
- NBC basketball analyst Steve Jones, referring to
Rick Mahorn of the Detroit Pistons

In ice hockey or football, court sense is called "seeing the field." In golf, it's referred to as course management. In baseball, it's field sense.

Sometimes it's easier to say what court sense *isn't* than to say what it is. To illustrate, I'd like to use an example that was given to me by a college coaching friend of mine. The names of the schools have been changed to protect the embarrassed.

With six seconds left on the clock, the Ben Franklin Lightning Rods were down by one with the ball out of boundS at center court. As the official handed the ball to the inbounder, the Rods set a double screen just above the top of the circle. Coming up from the baseline, their best shooter ran off of the screen. His defender, a young man playing for the George Washington Cherry Trees, was unaffected by the screen. He stayed tight on his opponent's hip and sliced between his man and the passer to intercept the ball. As the clock ticked toward the buzzer, the Cherry Tree drove the length of the floor for a two point lay-up, to put George Washington up by three with several ticks left on the clock.

1

The Cherry Trees immediately begin jumping for joy, seemingly oblivious to the fact that in college basketball, the clock automatically stops on any score in the last minute. As the Cherry Trees celebrated, a Ben Franklin player inbounded the ball, passing to a wide-open teammate just outside the three-point arch at the other end of the court. However, instead of shooting what could have been the tying three-pointer, the player drove in for two. He scored just before a George Washington player, in an apparent effort to foul him, ran him down. The foul was meaningless, however, as the buzzer had already sounded, leaving the Cherry Trees to win by one.

As my friend noted, this had to be an NCAA record for most dumb plays made by two teams in the last 0:06 of a game. Some of the mistakes included:

- The outside defender on the double screen and the defender on Ben Franklin's best shooter were supposed to switch, but didn't.

- The Ben Franklin receiver did not come to the ball, which, when coupled with a soft pass from the inbounder, allowed the George Washington defender to step between and intercept.

- After the interception, when he could have dribbled out the clock, the interceptor instead drove in for two points, giving the opposing team enough time for another play.

- George Washington players on the floor and on the sideline began to celebrate, thinking the game was won, when in fact there were still three seconds left to play.

- (This includes one player from the bench who came 20 feet onto the court, right in front of one of the officials, while the game was still in progress.)

- Instead of shooting for the tie, the Ben Franklin player drove in for two to seal the defeat.

2

- Trying to prevent a score that wouldn't have won the game anyway, a George Washington defender almost put the game in jeopardy by trying to foul on the Ben Franklin layup.

- Looking like an idiot, the George Washington coach ran out of the coaching box and all the way to mid-court, exhorting his team to get back on defense because the game wasn't over.

Of course, games like this aren't just restricted to basketball. The Los Angeles Dodgers had a prime example not too long ago when they played the Florida Marlins. The Dodgers opened the game without a first-base coach (he was in the bathroom), had a third baseman forget how many runners were on base, had a pinch hitter forget to touch second base, had a second baseman flub an easy grounder, and had a Gold Glove right fielder make one of the worst throws of his life. Needless to say, the Dodgers lost.

In both cases, you have to just kind of shake your head and wonder: "What were they *thinking*?"

They weren't thinking, of course, which brings us to the first crucial element of court sense: the ability to think.

TO THINK OR NOT TO THINK—THAT IS THE QUESTION

Words are failing me. I've never seen such courage, never seen such daring play, never seen such smart play, as well. What must be going through this young man's mind tonight?

> \- Ben Crenshaw, reporting on Tiger Woods'
> play at the 1997 Augusta Masters

How can you think and hit at the same time?

> \- Yogi Berra

On every pitch I was thinking about a thousand different things. If I didn't do a good job I might not pitch for a month, so I'd be afraid every time I got to a hitter. I'd say to myself, "If you walk this man, you're out of the ball game, so you can't afford to throw him a curveball." I'd worry about what the manager was thinking and what the coaches were thinking. Instead of concentrating on the batter, I'd be looking over my shoulder. Every time I would see the slightest flicker of movement in the bullpen, it would make me more nervous. I would lose my concentration and just throw the ball.

- Sandy Koufax, speaking of his days as a young pitcher

When I was researching this book, I had a long talk with John Wooden, the legendary UCLA basketball coach. The one issue we kept debating was whether players should be thinking on the floor. John kept saying, No, no, you don't want your players thinking about things. They should be so well drilled that the game just flows automatically.

It wasn't until later that I realized that the issue wasn't whether to think or not to think. The issue is what to think about and what not to think about. For example, Greg Maddux, the Atlanta Braves' pitcher, has said that he pitches best when he forgets about the batter and thinks only of the place he intends his pitch to go.

In basketball, the best free throw shooters usually do two things: 1) they follow the same routine every time, such as bouncing the ball three times and rocking on the balls of their feet; 2) they take the same stance every time. Following a procedure allows the shooter to free his mind from the distraction of worrying about, "Is my elbow pointing in the right direction?" or "Are my feet too far apart?"

You cannot shoot a free throw or any shot consistently well if you are thinking about the mechanics of your shot. I know from experience to look at a spot on the front rim of the basket and just let go, rather than look, think, and shoot. How come? I don't really know. But years of practice and zillions of shots have programmed my brain to do the job if my body is relaxed and prepared.

The point is, what you should *not* be thinking about are the mechanics of the game. You have to develop your skills and then go with them. As D.A. Weizburg said on the PGA tour, "You can't be thinking about eight different things. You've got to pick your target, make your decision, and go."

I believe that on the basketball court, there are two kinds of thinking: productive thinking and unproductive thinking. Unproductive thinking is thinking that distracts you. It makes you tense. It causes you to lose your confidence. No coach wants their players to be thinking unproductively.

Productive thinking, on the other hand, keeps you focused on the here and now. You're not thinking ahead to the end of the game, or thinking back to that mistake you made just a few minutes ago. You're concentrating on the matter at hand. You're thinking about the things you *should* be thinking about—like whether to pass or shoot, drive in or pull up, expend yourself or conserve energy.

It's a balancing act. Sometimes players short-circuit because they overload—they think too much. You have to find the balance that works for you.

THINKING SUCCESSFULLY ON THE COURT

Stockton is constantly thinking on the floor, and his grasp of the patterns and options of the Jazz offense is so complete that he sometimes throws passes to teammates before they are even open.

- from "PassMaster," by Phil Taylor,
Sports Illustrated, June, 1997

The challenge is always the same one—to see how good you can become. The difference now is that we have another area—the mind— to use to our best advantage.

- Robert Nideffer, Ph.D.,
Sports and Corporate Psychologist

One day, when Tiger was two, we were on the second hole at Navy Golf Course in Cypress, Calif. He had hit his ball into the trees to the right on a short par-4. I said, "What are you going to do, Tiger?" He looked and he said, "I can't hit the ball over those trees, Daddy, they're too tall." "Well, what else are you going to do?" I asked. "I can hit it between those trees, but I've got to keep it down. And there's a big sand twap." "O.K., what else can you do?" He looked to the left and said, "I can hit my ball out into the fairway, hit my next shot onto the green, and one-putt for a par." I said, "Son, that is course management."

- Earl Woods, *Training a Tiger*

The best players are not always the ones with the best skills. The best players are those who know how to think successfully. For all his skills with a golf club, Tiger Woods considers his ability to think his way around a course his biggest asset.

Successful thinkers aren't necessarily those people with the highest IQs. They're not always the ones who do well on tests, or who get straight-A's in school. Successful thinkers are those who think well in three different ways: analytically, creatively, and practically.

Analytical thinking is the kind of thinking you do when you need to solve a problem or judge how good an idea is. Another name for analytical thinking is "straight thinking." If you are going to paint a room and you need to know how many gallons of paint it takes to cover a 20 feet by 12 feet area, then analytical thinking is what you will use to figure out the answer. If you are an analytical thinker, you will probably do well in school because analytical thinkers tend to be good at taking tests. However, once you get out of school, analytical thinking might not be as useful to you as the ability to think creatively or practically.

Creative thinking is the ability to think of good ideas. Creative thinkers are willing to experiment and take risks. Creative thinking is "zigzag" thinking, as opposed to straight thinking. In creative thinking, there is seldom one "right" answer.

When I think of creative thinking, I am reminded of a problem that is often used to illustrate what creative thinking is all about. The goal is to connect the nine dots below, using no more than four straight lines, and without lifting your pen off the paper.

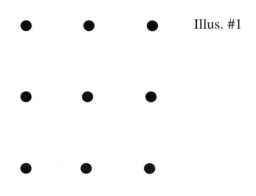

Illus. #1

Generally, people have a lot of difficulty trying to solve this problem. That's because they feel they need to keep their lines within the square created by the dots. The correct approach (below) shows that being creative sometimes means "thinking outside the lines" of a problem.

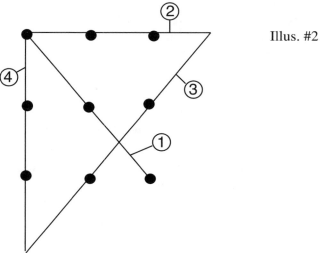

Illus. #2

Creative thinking is usually used to do one of two things:

(1) Make small changes in the existing way of doing something.
(2) Solve problems where straight thinking does not work.

For example, let's say you're not making your free throws. You experiment a little bit, and discover that by moving your hand six inches forward you eliminate a potential hitch in your shot. By making a small change in an existing way of doing something, you solve your free-throw problem.

Another example: You're coming down the court on the fast-break. It's three on two and the defense is set. You can give it up, barrel through out of control, or come up with some creative solutions—such as looking for the trailer, doing a crossover dribble, and heading for the second defensive player on the way to screen for his jump shot or a pick-and-roll.

The third element of successful thinking is the ability to think practically. Practical thinking is what you do when you take your ideas and apply them to your everyday life. You use practical thinking to execute your ideas.

When you think "successfully," you combine your analytical, creative, and practical skills. When I picture successful thinking on the basketball court, I am reminded of something that happened during one of my games at Stanford. We were playing the University of San Francisco before the largest crowd on the West Coast at that time (18,000 at the Cow Palace). I—all 5'8" of me—was driving the baseline from the left side of the basket, which was being guarded by 6'10" College Player of the Year and future NBA Hall-of-Famer Bill Russell.

Dribbling with my left hand, I headed for a reverse lay-in under the basket. As I went under the basket, I shifted the ball to my right hand and laid it down on the floor while continuing to drive under the basket for the reverse lay in. My center, Russ Lawler, whom I knew I could always count on to be alert, calmly reached down (while all other eyes were on me), picked up the ball and put it in.

Now, let's look at how I applied the three different kinds of thinking to solve this problem:

Analytical (recognizing the problem): I was 5'8." Bill Russell was 6'10." I recognized that trying to score over him wasn't going to work.

Creative (thinking of a way to get it done): If I couldn't get the ball to the hoop myself, maybe someone else could do it. However, the defenders would probably be expecting a pass. Was there some other way I could get the ball to a teammate?

Practical (executing the play): I laid the ball down and Russ did the rest.

Not only was I using my court sense, but Russ was using his. If he had not responded the way he did, my efforts probably would have resulted in a senseless turnover. However, I had conditioned him to expect the unexpected from me—which is exactly what he did.

If this sounds too confusing, don't worry. When you first learned how to dribble a ball, it probably didn't feel very natural to you, either. But just as you developed skills like dribbling and passing, you can also develop the thinking part of your game so that it becomes second nature. After all, your brain is a muscle much like any other muscle on your body—the more you use it, the easier it gets.

UNDERSTANDING THE GAME

Understanding the game can compensate for deficiencies that come with age. That explains why Dennis Rodman, 35, Charles Barkley, 34, and Dikembe Mutombo, 30, rank first, third, and fifth in rebounding [during the 1996-97 season]. Younger opponents might have more spring in their legs, but they haven't mastered the art of positioning and anticipating how the ball will carom off the backboard.

- Roscoe Nance, USA Today

Even when he was a teenager, Tiger Woods' power and shot-making skill ranked him with the world's best golfers. Now 21, he has added the mental game.

He thinks, therefore he wins.

- from an Associated Press article following Tiger Woods' victory at the Western Open

In his book, *Think to Win: The Strategic Dimension of Tennis,* Allen Fox talks about how he used to watch a regular match played between a professor of social science at Pepperdine University, and former UCLA and Pepperdine men's basketball coach Jim Harrick. The professor had obviously had many tennis lessons, whereas Harrick played "like a basketball player who had recently been given a racket as a gift and was enthusiastically trying it out." Surprisingly, Harrick usually won these matches. Fox went on to explain why:

> As I watched the mystery gradually resolved itself. Jim knew exactly what he was doing and the professor was just hitting shots.

9

The professor was oblivious to the percentages and invariably whacked balls hard and near the lines....Jim dinked the ball in the court, ran down enough of the professor's shots to give the professor a chance to miss, and put away enough volleys to keep the professor off balance. Jim understood how to cover up his own weaknesses and take advantage of his opponent's. The professor, meanwhile, relied solely on his strokes.

In basketball—as in tennis, or golf, or any other sport—if you want to be able to play to your full potential, it's not enough just to be a good shot-maker. As John Yandell of the *San Francisco Chronicle* wrote: "It doesn't matter how great your strokes might be if you never wind up getting into position to hit them." In other words, you have to understand how to use your shots in order to win. After all, anyone can learn how to sink a basket, if they practice long enough. The hard part is learning how to use your skills effectively.

Understanding the game means knowing:

- When to shoot the ball
- What kind of shot to use (i.e., a jump hook, a bank shot)
- How to shoot the ball
- When to pass the ball
- When to choose one option over another
- What it means when you talk about spacing, positioning, timing, angles vs. arches
- How to play "percentage" basketball

A lot of times, understanding the game is just knowing the little things—like knowing that you should hold your hands straight up and not attack when you're blocking a shot under the basket, or knowing that you can't get emotional when blocking a shot, because you'll probably swat the ball out of bounds instead of tipping it to a teammate. It's knowing that when you're attempting to feed the post, you're better off lobbing or bouncing a pass than throwing a chest level pass that can be easily intercepted. It's knowing that you don't save a ball from going out of bounds at the defensive end of the court, because more often than not you'll save it into an opponent's hands for an easy bucket.

Understanding the game also means knowing what strategy will allow you to make the most of your own physical talents. Jeff Hornaceck of the Utah Jazz has said that when he was a kid, he knew he wasn't going to be tall enough to be able to rely on his height to see him through as a basketball player. So if he was going to be able to continue playing the game he loved, he figured he'd better develop a specialty. What Hornaceck did was to spend hours practicing hard, off-the-wall shots. Shots on the run. Shots falling down. Shots off-balance. Perfecting that strategy has enabled Jeff Hornaceck to continue to play in a game where most of the players are much more physically gifted than he is.

Understanding the game means having a feel for the game. This usually comes with experience.

When Keith Van Horn, the University of Utah player who was drafted second in the 1997 draft, decided to stay in college for his senior year, a lot of people thought he was making a big mistake. But after completing an outstanding senior season, Van Horn said, "I really have a better understanding of the game. I'm able to recognize things much better on the court. I think that just comes from experience."

Tim Duncan, the Wake Forest All-American and number-one draft pick, also recognizes the value of experience. In a column that he wrote for *USA Today,* Duncan said:

> Physical and mental maturity—two qualities widely displayed during the Finals—are two key reasons why I opted to stay at Wake Forest rather than enter the NBA draft either of the last two seasons. While I might have been ready on a talent basis, I felt additional preparation in college was necessary for me to flourish in an 82-game schedule. Four years of college yielded more than a prestigious degree from Wake Forest; it afforded me a stronger, more durable game—on and off the court.

When you understand the game, it becomes second nature to you. You are able to comprehend and put together all aspects of the game—the mental, the social, and the physical—in a way that makes the whole (the team) greater than the sum of its parts (the players). I think this is one reason why the Utah Jazz were almost able to take the title away from the Chicago Bulls in the 1997 and 1998 NBA Finals. The Jazz may not have any single superstar player like Michael Jordan (Karl Malone's MVP notwithstanding), but they do have several very good players who know how to work together to take the team to a higher level. The Jazz, as a team, have excellent court sense—which is why you will notice me using them so often as an example.

Understanding the game is more than knowledge of how the game works. It is also knowledge of how *people* behave in a given situation. When you understand what a player is likely to do in a given situation—whether it's a teammate or an opponent—then you can anticipate their play instead of just reacting to it.

Michael Jordan continues to be an outstanding player because his understanding just keeps getting sharper and sharper. During the 1996-97 season, Michael said, "I know my teammates better and they know me. I also understand the game better than I ever did and I can see the court better than ever before. I'm making better decisions in given situations." That kind of understanding helped lead the Bulls to their sixth NBA championship.

Clyde Drexler, an NBA star for many seasons who's been around long enough to know what he's talking about, described it like this:

> You've got to know guys' mind-sets. Is this guy a shooter? Is he a passer? You've got to know every player's identity, and you've got to know it quickly. Is he more inclined to drive, or is he looking to dish? Some point guards are more inclined to look for their own shots. Most point guards will only look to pass. If you can play the lanes, then you throw off the whole play because they're not really looking at you. You just got to know the psychology of the game.

During my sophomore season at Stanford we were playing a conference game against USC. I noticed early in the contest that when I would make a defensive fake against my man, their point guard and best ballhandler, he would turn his back to me with the dribble. I filed that information away, and then, with less than 15 seconds to go in the game and the score tied, I made my move. I initiated a steal off his dribble because he did as I had observed earlier in the game—he turned his back to me to protect the ball. I continued around him to where the ball was exposed on the other side. It was an easy steal for the game-winning lay in.

A similar steal occurred during Game Four of the 1997 NBA Finals. The Chicago Bulls were ahead 73-69 with 1:45 to play. Michael Jordan had the ball, and just as he started to whirl toward the lane, John Stockton came from behind on the left side and picked Jordan clean. Stockton went on to score two points (on free throws) at the other end, and the Utah Jazz went on to win the game. Stockton, never one to blow his own horn, said, "It was kind of lucky timing." But Stockton's teammate, Karl Malone, disagreed. As Malone later explained it, Jordan had a habit of making that particular move in that particular situation. Stockton picked up on that and put that knowledge to good use.

That same Bulls-Jazz game also provided an excellent example of understanding your teammates. With less than a minute on the clock, Jordan's straight-away jump shot hit the rim of the basket and bounced off. Stockton got the rebound and immediately looked down court, where Jordan and Malone were in a footrace for the Jazz basket. Stockton took a dribble, then heaved the ball down the court. As Stockton later said, "If you could have suspended time right then, when the ball was in the air, [Utah coach] Jerry [Sloan] probably would have strangled me."

But Stockton knew Malone, and Malone knew Stockton. "I... knew that if anybody could get that pass to me, it was Stock." Malone said. "When he threw it, I thought, 'Well, Stock doesn't throw bad passes, so I must be open.'" Malone was open—barely—and he turned the bomb into a layup and a 74-73 lead. Stockton later admitted that if it had been anyone but Malone, he probably wouldn't have thrown the ball. But because he knew what Malone was capable of, he knew that the play could work.

When you understand the game, that means you know how to play *even when you don't have the ball.* You'd be surprised at how many players cannot play without the ball. All great players can. Players who know what to do, where to go, how to cut, how to set a screen or find a way to get an offensive rebound—these are the players who make themselves useful to the rest of the team. Many, many of today's players are very good with the ball and very poor without it. It's a mind thing.

You could say that what you do when you have the ball depends heavily on your athleticism, but what you do when you don't have the ball depends mostly on your court sense. In tennis, for example, do you stop playing once you hit the ball over the net? Of course not. Hitting the ball over the net is the easy part.

Can you learn to play without the ball? Sure, but it's not simple. Anytime you take away what you're good at and force yourself to rely on other skills, you're going to be uncomfortable for a while. For example, one highly successful Big Ten coach routinely makes dunking off-limits for the first three weeks of fall practice. His players hate it. It takes their game away from them, because they haven't yet developed skills beyond athleticism. They haven't yet developed an understanding of the game that allows them to play differently when needed.

You will find that the less understanding you have of the game, the less able you are to make changes in your game when you need to. Just look at Venus Williams. Williams is a young tennis player who is rising quickly through the tennis rankings. One of the reasons for this is that Venus Williams is a big girl who, because of her size, can hit the ball very hard. However, strength isn't everything. In her first Wimbledon match, Williams started well, easily overpowering her opponent with her strong shots. But then Williams' opponent changed her strategy. Playing the kind of "percentage" tennis that we talked about at the beginning of this section, she forced Williams into making numerous errors. Meanwhile, Venus Williams—deprived of her biggest weapon—didn't know what to do. She kept on trying to overpower her opponent, and eventually she lost the match.

A little further ahead in this book, under the section on "Learn to Think the Game," we'll talk more about what is involved in understanding the game and what kinds of things you can do to increase your understanding. For now, I'll just close with this saying from

What Court Sense Is...and Isn't

Johann Wolfgang Von Goethe: "Whatever you cannot understand, you cannot possess."

GETTING THE BIG PICTURE

I think he is one of these people who processes information very quickly. On the basketball court, he has the ability to see it happen before it happens.

- Deborah Best, chairwoman of theWake Forest
psychology department and academic advisor to
No. 1 draft pick Tim Duncan

I skate to where the puck is going to be, not to where it has been.
- Wayne Gretzky, New York Rangers

Written Chinese uses thousands of characters and symbols to communicate ideas. For example, the symbol for "seeing" is not just an eye, but an open eye atop two legs. Why is the eye on legs? Well, what can an eye with legs do that an eye without legs can't do? The Chinese eye is a metaphor for walking around situations, or looking at things from all angles. For thousands of years, the Chinese realized that people with fixed vision become inflexible and intolerant thinkers ("That's the way it is and nothing you say will change it.") The Chinese believe, however, that there is a more flexible, or fluid, way of looking at things.

Court sense includes the ability to "get the big picture." It means, literally, being able to see the whole court—as Michael Jordan mentioned earlier. But more than that, it means being able to process all the information your mind is receiving.

That can be hard to do. After all, you have the crowd screaming and yelling, you have a lot of movement taking place on the court, you have your defensive or offensive strategies to worry about, *and* you have to be alert as to what the other team is doing. It's a lot of information to take in all at once, especially if you haven't had that much experience. It can be very easy to get confused or miss a play.

Even the best players sometimes find it hard to get the big picture on the court. Tim Duncan wrote about the difficulty he had in understanding the NBA's "illegal defense" rule:

> While I am confident in my education and intelligence, I must confess I have rarely experienced anything as perplexing as illegal defense. Apparently, where other basketball courts are pretty much self-evident, NBA courts have all kinds of imaginary lines.
>
> For example, if your opponent is above the left top imaginary line and you are defending him, it is illegal to put a foot into the center imaginary line and below the other imaginary line. I've always thought of myself as reasonably imaginative, but give me a break!
>
> What if my imaginary line differs from the correct imaginary line? How imaginative is a line everybody (except me) knows about anyway? As I was getting a crash course in illegal defense, one thing became painfully clear: I do not understand illegal defense. Perhaps once I am officially inaugurated into the NBA, all those imaginary lines will miraculously appear before my eyes.

In a seminar I once gave, I asked a group of young people to draw a picture of their minds. Afterwards, we taped the pictures on the wall. The best one was a picture of an iceberg—the point being that most of us only use a small part of our brains. Like an iceberg, 80-90 percent our mind's potential is hidden. The average human brain has several billion times the storage capacity of any computer. Again, though, it's not enough to just store information ("Their weakest defender is on our best shooter; their center is slow to help on the weak side") in your brain. In order to develop court sense, you need to put that information to use. You need to figure out what the information means to the game ("Hey! I'm double-teamed, so that leaves so-and-so wide open. I'll get the ball to him and let him shoot").

In football, the quarterback needs to be able to take in the entire field at a glance. He needs to be able to instantly read the defense and make decisions based on what he sees. In basketball, every player needs to be a quarterback.

MAKING GOOD DECISIONS

Before Brad and I started working together, I had matches that were as good as I'll ever have. But day-in, day-out consistency wasn't there. I never had to think about anything before. I just went out there and played, figuring I was going to win. But when Brad played, he had to figure out a way to win every time. He had to think it through, and that court sense is something he's helped me with.
> \- Andre Agassi, talking about his coach, Brad Gilbert

He is so intelligent. He is a standout because he plays with his brain. He can adjust to any situation, and that's why he's such a standout.
> \- River Rouge (Michigan) basketball coach LaMonte Stone,
> praising high school star, Shane Battier

I mentioned some things that are important to me: to be a smart team, to be able to do certain things well. Basically, it was football things, like not to be heavily penalized, know how to use the clock, have players who could make decisions the coach would make without having the coach tell him to make them.
> \- Bill Parcells, head coach of the New York Jets

Court sense requires the ability to make good decisions in different kinds of situations. Not only do you have to be able to make good decisions, but you have to make them quickly. The faster and better you can make decisions, the higher will be your quality of play.

Basically, your goal as a player should be to make the highest percentage play every time you make a decision. If you decide to shoot a three-pointer, it shouldn't be because you're a good three-point shooter and the more shots you make the better you'll look to all those scouts out there. It should be because in that game, in that situation, taking the three-pointer is your team's best opportunity to score in the time that you have left on the shot clock.

Of all sports, wrestling is the one that probably gives the best example of having to make good, fast decisions. In amateur wrestling, the athlete who thinks is the one who wins. Strength and speed help, but when you wrestle, you're involved in dozens of instantly changing situations. You have to make decisions based on these situations. The wrestler who makes the best decisions the fastest usually wins.

Decision-making is a learned skill. It begins with having confidence in yourself. And where does confidence come from? It comes from competence, which means the ability to do something well. When you master the fundamentals of basketball—when you become competent at the game—then you gain the confidence you need to make good decisions. (We'll talk more about confidence.)

Even the most athletic player has to gain confidence and learn how to make good decisions. Just because Kobe Bryant was good enough to go straight from high school to the Los Angeles Lakers doesn't mean he didn't have anything to learn. Bryant's playing often showed his inexperience. However, by the time the Lakers made it to the Western Conference semifinals in 1997, Kobe noted that his confidence and decision-making had improved considerably. "My decision-making has improved. The more I would go through, the more I would see, the more I improved. I trust my decisions now. When I first started playing point guard, I didn't now how to run the offense all that well. I feel better now."

Sometimes athletes think that their coach should be the one to make all the decisions. (Sometimes coaches think the same thing.) However, that kind of attitude can get you in trouble, both now and later. Right now, not being able to make decisions on the court will keep you from being a good player. It will keep you dribbling the ball as time runs out because you don't know whether you should pass or shoot. Later, it will turn you into the kind of person who would rather have someone else make the decisions, so if anything goes wrong, you can blame them.

Someone once said that coaches should use chess games as a practice tool, to see how well their athletes can think in fluid situations. That's not such a bad idea. When you play chess, you learn how one move affects several pieces. Chess teaches you to be flexible. Flexibility, or the ability to make adjustments, is a big part of being a successful athlete and a happy, healthy person. As a psychologist and counselor, I have worked with hundreds of people whose biggest problem was their lack of flexibility. When something unexpected happened to them, they just couldn't adjust to it, and it messed up their whole lives.

What Court Sense Is...and Isn't

There's a story that illustrates just how important it is to be able to adjust to the unexpected. Some scientists were studying North American beavers to discover how much of their behavior is learned and how much is instinct. As you may know, beavers build dams in streams to form a small lake. Along the bank of this lake, beavers dig a tunnel leading to an underwater cave. They then store food in the cave to eat during winter.

But how do beavers get out of the cave in the winter, when the lake is frozen? Well, the river isn't frozen all the way through. Deep underneath the ice, the water is still moving. There is one spot where the currents keep the ice from freezing all the way. Beavers instinctively know where this spot is, and build the dam and the cave entrance in just the right position.

However, the group of beavers that the scientists were studying ran into trouble when it came to finding the water's opening. Maybe the current changed, changing the location of the hole. When one of the beavers swam out of the tunnel, instead of going to the hole, he banged up against thick ice. The hole was less than three feet away, but he would not go to it. The people tried to get the beaver to come over to the hole, but he wouldn't. It returned to its cave, and day after day, repeated the same behavior. In the spring, the scientists dug up the cave and found the bodies of two baby beavers and their parents. They had starved to death.

You see, the beaver's brain is hard-wired. It is programmed to do what it is supposed to do, and it can't adjust to unexpected events—like the hole not being where it should be. The beaver just does the same thing over and over again, because that's what beavers do.

But that is not what basketball players do—not the good ones, anyway. Good players have the ability to solve problems on the court. They identify problems and quickly adjust. They use their court sense to help them make game-winning decisions.

BEING A TEAM PLAYER

The individual isn't important in a basketball game.
          - Bernie Bickerstaff, coach of the Washington Wizards

Court Sense

Good teams have good players mixed with role players, but we have no role players.

- Rony Seikaly, talking about his former team,
the Golden State Warriors

I don't let the trade rumors or the critics or anything bother me. I know who I am, and I know what I can do.

- Scottie Pippen

Part of court sense is knowing what your role is on the team, and filling it. Not everyone can be or needs to be a superstar. In fact, it is often someone other than the superstar who holds the key to success. A game or series can swing easily on the fortunes of a player of lesser talent or fame. Every team has that one guy who needs to step up to make his squad successful.

There's a reason why Michael Jordan was so emphatic about having Scottie Pippen playing alongside him on the Chicago Bulls. Pippen is a great example of a team player. While Michael grabs the headlines, Scottie quietly goes about his job.

A team player contributes regardless of how he shoots on a given night, or even regardless of how many points his man scores. Good players make it tough for the other team to score. A team player helps his teammates stop their men, or helps them score more. He contributes in ways that the average fan never notices or thinks about.

Jeff Hornacek is a good example of that kind of player. During Game 4 of the NBA Finals, as Karl Malone was about to shoot two crucial free throws, Hornacek saw Scottie Pippen heading in Malone's direction. Pippen had made a crack at Malone earlier in the series (about the "Mailman not delivering on Sunday") right before Malone missed two free throws. Hornacek didn't want the same thing happening again. The fans probably didn't even notice Hornacek quietly stepping in front of Pippen, trying to protect Malone from any distracting comments. To Hornacek , his role as a team player means doing more than just trying to score points.

I member one year when USF played LaSalle for the NCAA championship. Tom Gola was the big star for LaSalle, and he was just a marvelous basketball player. But who did USF guard him with? K.C.

Jones. At first, that didn't make sense to a lot of people, since one of Jones' teammates was Bill Russell—arguably the greatest defensive player of all time. I'm sure many fans thought, "Hey, we should put Russell on Gola. He's our best guy!"

However, the coach's strategy was to have Jones aggressively attack Gola. Once Gola would beat Jones, he would still have to contend with Russell. By the end of the game, Jones and Russell had played their roles successfully. Gola was worn out and USF won the championship.

Team players know how to make their teammates better. I had a teammate in college who was an outstanding ballplayer (he competed in the 1956 Olympics as a member of the U.S. basketball team). However, in my opinion he was never a great player in any contest until he got his 15 points. So I would work my tail off to get him his 15 points so he would settle down to the job at hand—which was winning the game.

There are plenty of examples of what happens to a team when you have lots of talent but not much team spirit. The Golden State Warriors were loaded with talent, but didn't perform well during the 1995-96 season. Their center blamed the team's poor chemistry. "On the court, everybody's got different agendas. Sometimes you look at the teams we play and say, 'Not one of their players could start on our team.' Yet, they kick our butts."

Many people felt that part of Golden State's problem was point guard Tim Hardaway. What is the role of the point guard? To look for the pass first. To help his teammates score. However, as sportswriter Bruce Jenkins wrote about Hardaway:

> Most any time down the floor, he has two things on his mind: Pull up for the 23-footer, or drive through everybody for a lay up. It worked so...well for so many years, Hardaway didn't catch much flak for shirking his point guard responsibilities. But it is evident now, as Coach Adelman tries to rework the team's offensive philosophy, that Hardaway is caught between new information and his basic instincts. The Warriors, as presently constructed, don't need this. They need five guys who think like Chris Mullin, Joe Smith

and backup guard Jon Barry—think pass, then go for yourself if it's the better option.

When you're part of a team, your ultimate agenda should be to win—not to show everybody what a great player *you* are. In a four-game streak, Allen Iverson scored 44, 40, 44, and 50 points—becoming the first rookie to score 40 or more in four consecutive games. However, his team lost all four of those games. Jim Trotter commented: "He has so much talent, yet so little understanding. A point guard is supposed to be the central nervous system of a basketball team. He is supposed to control and regulate. Iverson wants to dominate....After a game earlier this season, Iverson said the 76ers needed to learn his game and feed off him. Actually, it should have been the other way around. He needs to learn his teammates' games and how to get the most out of each of them."

The first time former Utah Jazz head coach Frank Layden saw John Stockton play in person was at a tryout camp in Chicago, where many of the players were trying to make a name for themselves by shooting first and passing second. Layden said he didn't see anything special about Stockton at the time. His son Scott, who ultimately made the decision to draft Stockton, disagreed. "I saw a complete player," he said. "He was playing on a team with Kevin Willis, and he made Kevin Willis look like a real player. So, Kevin really owes Stockton. He doesn't know it, but he should give part of his paycheck to Stockton. Because Willis was running the court, dunking the ball and Stock was dishing it to him. If I remember back, Willis almost looked like Karl Malone."

Understanding the game, getting the big picture, making good decisions, and knowing your role—all these things are part of successfully thinking on the court. They are all part of court sense. If you're lucky, you were born with it. If you weren't born with it, you can still learn it. But you have to be willing to work at it. Are you ready to do that?

PART TWO

HOW DO YOU
GET COURT SENSE?

Chapter  2

LEARN TO LEARN

Players with court sense are made, not born (although it helps to inherit good peripheral vision). Learning court sense involves a lot of things—learning basketball fundamentals, learning how to be confident, and so on. But before I talk about any of these things, I want to spend some time giving you a few coaching tips on how to be a better learner. What we're about to talk about now is probably the most important part of this book, so don't even think about skipping over this section! What you learn here will not only help you become a better basketball player—it will help you become a better student of life.

BE WILLING TO LEARN

When the student is ready, the teacher will appear.

- Buddha

The readiness is all.

- William Shakespeare

Are you coachable? Before you can learn about something, you have to be open to learning. You have to be willing to learn. What does it mean to be coachable? It means:

You respect authority. You don't have to like your coach (or your math teacher or English teacher), but if you want to learn from them, you have to be respectful. You listen to what they say, instead of goofing around. You try to do the things they tell you to do.

You enjoy trying new things. If someone points out a flaw in your shooting mechanics, you don't automatically say, "I like my way better," just because you don't like changing things around.

You are open-minded. You realize you can learn valuable lessons from anyone, regardless of that person's age, sex, academic credentials, or social status.

You know how to listen. Listening means understanding, not just hearing. A good listener uses his eyes as well as his ears, avoids prejudging, and tests his understanding by asking questions and restating or rephrasing the message.

You are able to handle order and organization. One professional basketball player (a habitual problem-maker) got in trouble with his coach for missing yet another practice. His excuse? He went to the wrong gym. The coach's response was that it was the player's responsibility to know where practice was being held.

You can accept criticism. When someone criticizes you, you have two choices: to learn or defend. Most people choose to defend themselves against criticism, instead of trying to learn from it. You don't have to like criticism or agree with it, but learning to handle it is important.

Being coachable shows that you are a mature player. When Elvin Hayes was honored as one of the 50 greatest players in NBA history, he said some critical things about rookie point guard Allen Iverson. "Iverson plays like a runaway train," Hayes said. "The bottom line is what your team does, and his team is not doing anything. If he doesn't show respect for the top players, then maybe he should read up on them. His head is in the wrong place."

Elvin Hayes knew what he was talking about. When Hayes was a rookie, he thought he knew it all, too. He had a big ego and a reputation for doing his own thing. But the more Hayes matured and realized he *didn't* know it all, the better he played. "When I left basketball, I was much more humble than when I first came," Hayes said.

Being humble helped him to be coachable, and being coachable helped him to become the kind of ballplayer who would one day be recognized as one of the best.

WHY LEARNING IS IMPORTANT

The illiterate of the year 2000 will not be the individual who cannot read and write, but the one who cannot learn, unlearn, and relearn.
                                        - Alvin Toffler, author and futurist

Why is it so important to learn how to learn? Let's say your goal in life is to become the next Michael Jordan (or something pretty close to it). So all you have to be good at is basketball. Right? Wrong. In the first place, how are all those NBA scouts going to see you play if you're benched or ineligible because your grades aren't high enough?

Second, do you know what the odds are of making the NBA, even if you are a good basketball player? They are very, *very* small. No more than two percent of high school athletes make it in college sports; only one in 10,000 goes on to the pros.

But let's say you beat the odds and make it to the NBA. What are the odds that you'll become an elite player like Michael Jordan? It's more likely that you would become a journeyman player. In that case, don't plan on living off your millions once you retire. The majority of players who make the pros—in any sport—do not find themselves on easy street once their playing days are done. They still have to work in order to support themselves. And if the only thing they know how to do is play sports, then they have a lot of catching up to do. That's not fun when you're 35 and your career's over and everyone out in the real world is way ahead of you.

All right, now just for the sake of argument, let's say you do make the pros and you become the next Michael Jordan. Does that mean there's no need to keep on learning? If that were true, then why did Michael Jordan bother to earn a degree in geography two years after leaving North Carolina to turn pro? Why did Emmitt Smith, a first-round draft choice for the Dallas Cowboys, return to the University of Florida six years after he left? Then there's Ahmad Rashad, who earned a degree in sociology *24* years after leaving the University of Oregon. None of these men had a financial need to have these diplomas. But they recognized the importance of continually learning new things. That desire to exercise their mental muscles is part of what makes them such good athletes.

Because the world is constantly changing, there is no one subject or group of subjects where you can say, "I can just learn this well, then I'm set for life." Change is so rapid in the business world that almost every day presents you with new challenges. It's the same for our personal lives. Just look at how attitudes and beliefs on such issues as homosexuality and abortion have changed over the past 20 years. If you aren't able to continually learn about and adapt to the changes that will happen in your life, then you will find yourself being passed over by people who *are* able to learn. Being able to learn throughout life is a key to personal success.

YOU CAN LEAD AN ATHLETE TO THE FIELD, BUT YOU CAN'T MAKE HIM THINK

Who's responsibility is it to see that you learn? Your coach's? Your teacher's? Your parents'? No, their job is to teach you. It's your job to learn.

John Wooden's biggest emphasis as a coach was on learning the fundamentals of basketball. Players would do the same basic drills over and over until they could pretty much do them in their sleep. Many players found this incredibly boring...until they started winning championship after championship. Then they saw the value of doing all the "boring" stuff.

If you think learning is boring, it's probably because you either don't know much about the subject you're learning, or you can't see the importance of doing it. I'm reminded of a story a friend of mine tells. It seems that, growing up, she always thought of ballet as something that was boring and stuffy. The idea of sitting through a ballet performance was about as exciting to her as dental surgery.

Then, in college, my friend was roommates with a ballerina. "Getting a first-hand look at ballet was a real eye-opener for me," my friend said. "You see the hours and hours they put into rehearsal; you see the taped ankles and the swollen feet. Once you've seen the blood in their shoes, you can never look at ballet the same way again."

If learning is boring to you, it's probably because:

- You don't know enough about the subject.
- You don't give something enough time to become interesting.
- You don't have enough curiosity to explore something new.
- You're narrow-minded—you don't like the teacher so you
    decide you won't like the subject.
- You just plain don't like or care about much of anything.

Sometimes athletes use sports as an excuse to spend less time learning other things. At the first meeting of *Sports for Life, Inc.*, our non-profit organization dedicated to helping athletes make the most of their sports experience, I asked the members of the board of directors to go around the room and introduce themselves. As they did so, most of the board members talked about the great impact sports had on their lives. However, when we got to Frank Boren, a college classmate of mine and one of the country's leaders in the conservation movement (he served as executive director of the Nature Conservancy for many years), Frank said: "When I got cut from both the football and basketball teams (at Stanford), I discovered there was a library."

What Frank was saying was that it wasn't until he was finished with sports that he started to get interested in learning other things. Don't be like Frank. Don't ever use sports as an excuse to not learn. You will find that a library card will be more valuable to you than any credit card you will ever own.

Right now, the learning you do in school is so much easier than the learning you will have to do in real life. Most of the problems that your teachers give you are well-structured. If you follow a certain set of steps, you get the right answer. Real life problems—like how to choose the right career or the right marriage partner—are not so clearly laid out. And no matter how much you keep hoping someone will come along and solve the problem for you, it doesn't happen. You have to learn to solve the problem yourself. As one high school athlete said when talking about trying to balance school work with sports: "You can't depend on anyone [to do it for you]. You end up learning that there's no one out there who's really going to help you. Those little things can take you far in life."

BELIEVE YOU CAN LEARN

The growth of the human mind is still high adventure, in many ways the highest adventure on earth.

- Norman Cousins

"Hey, I want to learn!" you say. "And I've tried. But I'm just not good at it. I don't have the smarts."

Let me tell you about Robert Sternberg. Sternberg is a professor of Psychology and Education at Yale University. He's written numerous papers and books about thinking and learning. However, when Sternberg took his first psychology class in college, he only got a C. That was when he decided maybe he wasn't cut out to become a psychologist. So he switched his major to math, and did even worse. He switched back to psychology and later graduated with high honors.

In high school, Sternberg's French teacher told him he didn't have the natural ability to learn foreign languages. So he avoided language classes. Many years later, though, he got a job where he had to learn Spanish. He quickly learned the language, and now speaks it fluently.

Just because you may not have done well in a class or on a test doesn't mean you can't learn.

ROADBLOCKS TO LEARNING

There are a lot of things that make us believe we can't learn. In school, for example, you're constantly being told to learn stuff, but no one ever tells you *how* you're supposed to learn it. Take vocabulary tests. You're given a list of words and by Friday you're supposed to know how to spell them. But how do you go about learning these words? Do you write them over and over? Do you have your mom ask you how to spell them? Do you stare at the paper until the words somehow sink into your brain? Or do you spend so much time worrying about the test that you never manage to learn the words?

When you get so nervous about learning something that you have trouble learning it, it's called "learning anxiety." Learning anxiety can leave you with bad feelings about learning—and those feelings keep you from seeing learning as something fun and exciting.

There are six major fears people have about learning:

(1) **I don't understand what I'm learning.** It's not that you *can't* understand—you just don't understand. This might be because your learning style is different from your teacher's teaching style (we'll talk more about this later).

(2) **I'm not a person who can learn this subject.** There's usually something you think you can't learn (like Robert Sternberg thought he couldn't learn foreign languages). Again, with the right kind of teaching, you probably can learn it. Find someone who can teach you in a way that makes sense to you.

(3) **I don't know how to learn this.** If you don't know how, then you probably need to have more direction. Ask your teacher or coach to spell things out for you, or give you clearer guidelines. Or ask them to tell you how *they* went about learning something—like how to find their best shooting position, or figure the square root of 16.

(4) **I don't remember what I'm learning.** There are things you can do to help you remember better. We'll talk about this when we talk about ways to improve how you learn.

(5) **I feel embarrassed that I don't already know this.** An 11-year- old girl took a dance class for the first time. All the other girls in the class already had several years of dance lessons. "I could see on her face that she was just embarrassed to death," said the girl's dance teacher. "She felt like everyone else knew it all, and she didn't know anything." What's worse? Saying, "I don't know, but I want to learn," or saying, "I don't know and I don't care enough to learn."

(6) **There's too much to learn.** Yes, there is. So don't think about that (it's called "information overload"). Instead, focus on what you have learned and how you're using the things you've learned.

YOU'RE ONLY AS SMART AS YOU WANT TO BE

Unless you try to do something beyond what you have already mastered, you will never grow.

- Ralph Waldo Emerson

One of the biggest blocks to learning is believing that being a good thinker is something that comes naturally. In other words, you believe you're either born with thinking skills or you're not. Well, sometimes being a good thinker does come naturally. Sometimes being a good basketball player comes naturally. But most of the time, basketball is something you have to work at if you want to do well. It's the same with thinking. The harder you work at it, the better you can get. In other words, *you* control whether you are someone who learns, or some-one who doesn't.

Believing that you are capable of exercising control over things that affect your life (like school or basketball) is called self-efficacy. You don't have to remember the term, but you do need to remember what it means. Self-efficacy is a kind of self-confidence. It means believing that you can do something.

For example, when a pitcher is looking at bases loaded and a 3-2 count, and he believes he can get the ball over the plate and not walk in the winning run, he is showing self-efficacy. When a gymnast be-lieves she can do a backward flip off the balance beam and land square on her feet, that is self-efficacy. That kind of belief is critical to actu-ally being able to carry out the action. If you don't believe you can do it, you probably won't be able to—even if you have the ability.

Some schools have started learning efficacy programs that teach kids that success doesn't come from having a natural ability to learn, but from something they can control through commitment and hard work. The basic belief behind these programs is that intelligence isn't something that is fixed, but can be developed. If you think, you can work hard, and as a result you'll get smarter.

If you believe that nothing you can do will make you any smarter, then you will be helpless to learn. You will stop trying. You have to believe that you can learn. Once you have that belief, you will find that:

- You try harder when confronted by obstacles.
- You abandon strategies that aren't working and try new strategies more quickly.
- You stay with the task longer before giving up.
- You set higher goals.
- You have more commitment to achieving goals.
- You set more challenging goals after your first goals are met.
- You expect to succeed.

All of these are things that will help you become a better basketball player and a better student. Ultimately, they will help you to become more successful in anything you do.

UNDERSTAND HOW YOU LEARN

Everyone learns differently. When you understand how you learn, then you will have a better idea of what you need to do to learn better.

First of all, what do you know about your brain? The human brain contains 10 to 20 billion brain cells and 50 to 100 billion neurons. Neurons are the things that carry signals from your brain to your body. Your brain weighs less than three pounds—about the same as a laptop computer. But there the similarity ends. Your brain has the capacity to store more information than all the libraries in the world.

It has been said that we only use about one percent of our brainpower. Now, however, scientists are saying that we use even less than that! As an athlete, you should become aware of the incredible power that lies within your brain. The untapped potential of your brain equals untapped potential to improve your game. Developing your thinking skills can lead to great results on the court.

Now, how does the brain work? Your brain is divided into two halves: left and right. The left side of your brain is the side that handles numbers, words, logic, lists, details. The right side handles pictures, imagination, color, rhythm, space. Most people generally use one side of their brain more than the other. For example, athletes tend to more often be "right brain" people. As a basketball player, you use your right brain when you "see the court," when you visualize sinking a free throw, and when you get into the rhythm of the game.

However, you will find that most of your classes in school put more value on "left brain" skills. That's one reason why athletes often do well in sports but not as well in the classroom. Nevertheless, you can strengthen your left brain function. Every time you do a math problem, write an essay, or make a list of things you need to do, you're doing a left brain exercise. And what happens when you exercise something? It gets stronger.

People who have been trained to use both sides of their brain have found that they can be five to 10 times more effective in their work. The more mental skills you use, the more creative you become.

YOUR LEARNING STYLE

We all have different styles of learning. A style is a way of doing something. Your learning style is not good or bad, just different. Some people like to work on several different things at once. Others need to start one thing and keep at it until they finish it. Some people like to work on their own; others do better in a group. One person may love structure in learning tasks; another may hate it. One person may enjoy new ways of doing things; another may fear them.

Some educators have said that our minds work much the same way as our government. There are three branches of government: legislative (Congress), executive (the President), and judicial (the Supreme Court). Each of these branches of government has a different job, or function.

Now, how does this apply to our minds? The *legislative* function of the mind is concerned with creating, designing, imagining, and planning. The *executive* function of the mind is concerned with starting and finishing a project. And the *judicial* function of the mind is concerned with judging, evaluating, and comparing. Mental self-government involves all three functions. However, in each person, one of the functions tends to be stronger than the others. I have a friend, for example, who is always coming up with ideas for new products or inventions—however, he never gets around to actually inventing any of these things. Another friend of mine doesn't have a creative bone in his body, but if you give him an assignment, you can depend on him to get it done. A third friend of mine is the one I go to when I want an opinion of something I'm working on. He is always able to look at what I'm doing and tell me if it's any good or not.

People can use more than one style—meaning you might think legislatively sometimes, and judicially other times—but we differ in our ability to switch among them. While no one relies only on a single style, some people are better than others at shifting back and forth.

Just as you need to be able to use both sides of your brain, you also need to develop ways to make the most of your particular learning style, while developing the ability to move from one style to another.

You also need to understand that a person's learning style influences how they teach. If your coach or teacher is a left brain, executive-style kind of learner, he or she will teach in that style. If you're a right brain, legislative kind of learner, you may have a hard time learning from them.

Does this mean you need to ask all the teachers in your school what their learning style is, so you can pick the ones who match your style and do better in their classes? No, of course not. The point I'm trying to make is this: Don't get discouraged if you are trying hard to learn something and just aren't "getting" it. It doesn't mean you're stupid and it doesn't mean you can't learn.

Let me tell you about Brian McKenzie. McKenzie was a star football player in high school, with dreams of playing for a Division 1-A college team. And they all wanted him—Florida, Florida State, Michigan. There was just one small problem. McKenzie couldn't score high enough on his SAT to get into one of those schools. He wasn't stupid. He had maintained a B-minus average through high school. He just had the unfortunate luck to be one of those people who don't test well.

But Brian McKenzie didn't give up. He enrolled in a junior college in Arizona, became a JC All-American and got his associate's degree. He went on to become a leading rusher at Brigham Young

University and a prospective NFL draft pick. Even more, he made the commitment to finish school, despite the obstacles. As Brian said, "I want to prove...that you don't have to be a brainiac to get a degree."

WHAT DOES "INTELLIGENT" REALLY MEAN?

Learning styles have to do with how you learn; intelligence has to do with how you *use* what you learn.

There are a lot of different ways to be intelligent. Our educational system mainly buys into one—analytical intelligence, which is measured by tests, scores, etc. However, if "intelligence" means the ability to solve problems or create things, then there are many different kinds of intelligences. For example:

• **Linguistic intelligence** is the ability to use language well. Poets and writers have linguistic intelligence.

• **Logical-mathematical** intelligence has to do with logical thinking, mathematics, and scientific ability. An accountant is someone who has logical-mathematical intelligence.

Linguistic and logical-mathematical intelligence are the ones we traditionally have rated the highest. Do well in these and you'll ace your SATs. How well you do after school, however, depends on how well you use your other intelligences. Spatial intelligence is the ability to form a mental model of a spatial world and to be able to maneuver and operate using that model (engineers, painters, and athletes have spatial intelligence). Athletes also have bodily-kinesthetic intelligence—that's the ability to solve problems or fashion products using your whole body, or parts of the body. *Inter*personal intelligence is the ability to understand other people. *Intra*personal intelligence is ability to understand yourself.

One type of intelligence people talk a lot about these days is emotional intelligence. That's the ability to control your emotions, to understand others, and handle relationships. What kinds of things do you have to know in order to be emotionally intelligent? First, you must know your own emotions and how to manage them. That includes the ability to control impulses, wait for what you want, and handle life's ups and downs. Second, you need to understand how other people feel. You also need to know what it takes to have successful relationships with others (parents, teammates, girlfriends/boyfriends, etc.). Emotional intelligence is often pointed to as a sign of maturity.

The tools that we usually use to measure intelligence—like IQ tests, SATs, and so on—really aren't a good measure of how intelligent a person is. That's because many areas of intelligence are not represented on these tests. For example, an IQ test may show that you know how to diagram a compound sentence, but it can't show that you also have the ability to put people at ease as soon as you meet them. In today's world, that second skill is often more valuable than the first!

Schools are wising up, though. They're using music, art, computers, and things like that to bring out the different kinds of intelligence that students may have.

Of course, I believe that sports can also be used to encourage intelligent behavior. How many times have you heard someone say, "He's really a smart player." When I hear that, I know they're describing someone with court sense.

LEARNING IS ACTIVE

Movement is the door to learning.

- Paul E. Dennison

Peter Senge, who wrote a book called *The Fifth Discipline*, said that most people believe that learning is taking in information, and when we can repeat back the information we have taken in, then we have learned. However, he notes that that's not how we learned to ride a bike, or walk, or talk. After all, your parents didn't sit you down with a grammar book when you were one and say, "Here, read this. We'll expect to hear you speaking complete sentences by the end of the day." You learned to talk by talking. You learned to walk by walking.

We learn by doing. One of the reasons "school" learning can be boring is that taking in information is passive. "But real learning," Senge says, "is always 'in the body.' It is intimately connected to action."

We learn when we are able to make the information we receive mean something to us. For example, when I first started learning how to use my computer, I sat down, read all the instructions, and didn't have a clue as to what to do next. *Really* learning how to use my computer has been a long and drawn-out process. It involves deciding what I need to know (such as how to delete a file), reading the information, and then carrying out the action. Until I actually *do* the thing on my computer, reading about it isn't very helpful. It's the action that helps me learn.

That is what's so wonderful about sports such as basketball. They are active learning. With every play, every shot, there is something to learn. You learn how people react to different situations. You learn how you react. You learn when it's okay to take risks, and when it isn't. You learn how to have confidence in yourself and others. You learn how to work together.

Learning is building on what you know. So you take the sport you know, and you learn from it.

IMPROVE HOW YOU LEARN

As I began writing this book, I had one major belief: that playing basketball could help you become a better thinker (and becoming a better thinker could help you become a better basketball player). Finding information to back that belief, however, was a different story. Then I met Art Costa, whose book *The School as a Home for the Mind* is in its fourth printing.

In his book, Dr. Costa lists 14 intelligent behaviors, or characteristics, that good thinkers have. These include persistence, flexibility, self-control (thinking before you act), cooperative thinking (teamwork), risk taking, and others.

Now, let me ask you: Can playing a sport such as basketball help you learn persistence? It certainty can. How about flexibility? Or self-control? Of course. Do you learn how to take risks when you play basketball? Do you learn teamwork? Yes, you can learn all of these things by playing basketball. You don't automatically learn them, however—it's something that you have to work at. But the better you get at teamwork, self-control, and so on, the better you get at thinking. And the better you get at thinking, the better you get at playing.

SIGNS OF INTELLIGENT LIFE

To improve how you learn, you need to behave intelligently. That doesn't mean you walk around quoting Shakespeare all the time. It means you act the way intelligent people act. You do the things intelligent people do. And when you are faced with a question or a problem for which you don't know the answer, you use what you've learned to solve it.

Basketball—or sports in general—is a great laboratory for learning how to think. Let's look at some sports examples of intelligent "behaviors."

Intelligent Behavior: Persistence. Dr. Costa says, "People who behave intelligently try to stick to a task until it is completed. They don't give up easily." They are committed.

Sports example: Michael Jordan was cut from his high school basketball team. "I was down about not making it for a while," he said, "and I thought about not playing anymore. Of course, I did keep on playing, and whenever I was working out and got tired and figured I ought to stop, I'd close my eyes and see that list in the locker room without my name on it, and that usually got me going again." Michael Jordan, like other great players, knows what it means to be committed.

Intelligent Behavior: Self-Control. Intelligent people think before they act.

Sports example: Although there are many examples of athletes who use self-control, it is the examples of ones who don't *use* self-control that we notice the most. Professional baseball player Roberto Alomar lost control and spit on an umpire. Mike Tyson lost control and bit Evander Holyfield's ear. As a result, both earned the scorn and disrespect of millions of people.

Intelligent Behavior: Listening to and Understanding Others.
Some psychologists believe that the ability to listen to and understand
others is one of the highest forms of intelligent behavior. Shortly
after Princess Diana died in a tragic car accident, I read an article that
said people never thought of Diana as very intelligent because she
didn't get good grades in school. However, Diana had a great ability
to reach out to people and connect with them emotionally. She had
emotional intelligence.

Sports example: How do you know when you've really understood what someone has said to you? Here's one example. On the
first day of practice, your coach explains his philosophies about winning, sportsmanship, teamwork, and stuff like that. That night, you go
home and share with your parents what your coach said—only you
don't use his words, you use your own words. You know you understand someone when you can tell what they're feeling just by watching the way they move or listening to the sound of their voice. Being
able to understand others is a key part of court sense. If you can sense
when a teammate or an opponent is full of confidence or when their
game is off, then you can play to that strength or weakness.

Intelligent Behavior: Cooperative Thinking (Teamwork). Earl
Nightingale, a famous motivational speaker, once said that "Getting
along well with other people is still the world's most needed skill."
Dr. Costa said that: "Humans who behave intelligently realize that all
of us together are more powerful than any one of us."

Sports Example: Again, the Utah Jazz are a good example of a
team that—together—does great things. In the 1997 off-season, the
Jazz lost only one of their free agents, even though most of them could
have signed with other teams at bigger salaries. To the Jazz, teamwork means more than just playing well together. Team owner Larry
Miller shared this example of what happens when a new player comes
to the Jazz: "Almost always when players get drafted or traded here
the reaction is almost always the same: 'Oh nuts.' I'll tell you what
happens is guys on our team get on the phone and call those guys and

welcome them to the team. I think we have something very special on this team that includes players, coaches and management that is a kind of camaraderie and a kind of common value system that I believe everyone buys into."

Intelligent Behavior: Flexibility. This is the kind of "zigzag" thinking that I talked about earlier. If something isn't working for you, you're open to trying new ways of doing things.

Sports Example: Sports, by its very nature, is unpredictable. Events change quickly and without warning, and if you're not flexible, you can be caught off-guard. For example, in 1988, a talented track and field athlete was on her way to Seoul to compete in the summer Olympics. At that time, her performance was close to the U.S. record. She was in an excellent position to contend for the medal. However, after the young woman arrived in Seoul, she was subjected to housing problems and unfamiliar food. And then, 15 minutes before the start of the last race, the officials announced there would be a long delay. All of these difficulties proved to be too much for the athlete. When the race was finally run, she was distraught, unfocused, cold, and nervous. Her lack of flexibility in being able to adapt physically and mentally to the changed circumstances resulted in a poor performance. Looking at the top three finisher's times, the young woman realized a medal would have been hers if she had just been able to run her normal race.

Intelligent Behavior: Being Aware of Your Own Thinking. The fancy name for this is "metacognition." It just means that you should be alert to how you think and whether you're doing good thinking or bad thinking. This process includes being able to:

- analyze what you know and what you need to know
- identify what information is missing and your plans for getting that information
- formulate your plan of action before you begin to solve a problem

- list the steps and tell where you are in solving a problem
- trace the detours or wrong turns you took on the road to solving the problem

Sports Example: An opponent is trash-talking you on the court. The more you hear, the angrier you get. Finally, you're so upset that you're about ready to take a swing at the guy. However, before you do, you realize: "Wait a minute—this kind of thinking won't help my game. What can I do to turn this around? I know that what he's trying to do is get me mad. How would he react if I don't get mad at all? I think I'll trying smiling at him every time he says something. Maybe that will throw *his* game off. Hey, it's working! He almost missed that pass!"

What you just did there was to: 1) describe what you know ("he's trying to get me mad"); 2) describe what you need to know ("how will he react if I don't get mad?"); 3) describe your plans for getting information you need ("I'll try smiling at him"); and 4) tell where you are in solving the problem ("Hey! It's working!").

Intelligent Behavior: Communicating Accurately. The better you are communicating with others, the fewer mistakes you and your team will make.

Sports Example: Allen Fox, a psychologist and championship tennis player, once wrote about a doubles tennis match he was a part of. Three or four times, Fox' partner, Larry Nagler, got them to break point and each time Fox missed the important service return. Fox said this happened about 10 times in one game, until he was so frozen by fear and embarrassment that he could hardly play. Fortunately, his partner continued to play well and they finally won. Fox said that the only reason he didn't fall apart completely was that Nagler was supportive and understanding. As Fox said, "*Never* lose sight of the fact that the overall objective is to communicate with your partner in such a way as to make him (or her) play his best. Make him feel good and the chances are he will play better."

Intelligent Behavior: A Sense of Humor. What does having a sense of humor have to do with being intelligent? It helps you get over your mistakes quickly, so you can move on with the game. A sense of humor helps you have a positive attitude, and a positive attitude is a winning attitude.

Sports Example: Casey Stengel was well loved as the longtime manager of the New York Yankees. However, as a player Stengel took a lot of abuse from the fans. On one occasion, Stengel had just about enough of the yelling and jeering. He caught a dove and brought it to the ballpark. Between innings he put the dove under his cap. When the fans started in on him, Stengel turned and tipped his cap to the crowd. Out flew the dove. Stengel could have let the crowd bring him down; instead, he lifted them up. That kind of attitude helped him achieve a long and successful career.

Intelligent Behavior: Asking Questions. One of the things that makes people different from animals or plants is our ability to question things. Intelligent people aren't afraid to ask questions.

Sports Example: Sometimes athletes expect their coach to do all their thinking for them. When you ask questions, however, that means you are thinking for yourself. Richard Williams, the father of tennis star Venus Williams, has tried hard to see that his daughter grows up to be a young woman who can take care of herself, instead of being a pampered athlete who expects everyone to take care of her. As Williams said, "Most of these kids go out there way too soon. They're kids in an adult world. It ain't fair. Once you go in, you can't stop it. It's impossible...But look what happens to these kids when they do go out there. Tennis kids are the worst socially developed children you'll ever see. No school. Can't spell well. Can't think well. Can't speak well. Their lives are all screwed up."

Intelligent Behavior: Applying What You Already Know to New Situations. Intelligent people learn from experience. They take what they learn in one situation and apply it to a new situation. My two-year-old grandchild, for example, learned what "hot" is when he accidentally learned against the warm oven door one day. Later, when I told him not to touch some running water because it was hot, he was able to remember what that meant to him. The ultimate goal of sports is for athletes to be able to apply the things they learn in sports to real-life situations.

Sports Example: A young man who had played football in high school and college left to serve a two-year mission for his church in Argentina. While the young man was walking along the street one day, his watch was stolen. As he ran after the thief, who was weaving down the street at a furious run, the young man thought, "Hey, this is just like football!" Using the skills he had learned, he brought down the thief with a flying tackle and retrieved his watch. Of course, transferring your learning from sports to the real world isn't always that easy. Sometimes you have to really work to make the connection. For example, a quarterback who is filling out a college application might write something like this: "As a quarterback, I have to be able to 'get the big picture' when I'm on the field. I have to see everything at a glance and make accurate decisions based on what I see. This is a skill that will help me do well as a business major. Business people have to be able to look at the competition and 'get the big picture.' Then they have to use that information to make good decisions."

Intelligent Behavior: Taking Risks. Intelligent people like to push their limits. As Frederick Wilcox said, "Progress always involves risk; you can't steal second base and keep your foot on first."

Sports Example: Dr. Costa uses Dick Fosbury as an example of someone who took risks and tried new things. In the early 1960s, Fosbury refused to high-jump like everyone else. Instead, he insisted on going over the bar backwards and head first. This technique came to be known as the "Fosbury Flop." It not only helped Fosbury win an Olympic gold medal, "It also became the standard practice for future athletes, who broke records with jumps that experts believed were unattainable."

Here's another creative example of how taking risks can pay off. An eight-man division Kansas high school football team scored a touchdown on a play suggested by one of the school's teachers. The play (which was cleared with the officials in advance) called for the team's quarterback and center to argue over whether the ball was the right one for the game. When the quarterback started for the sidelines as if to exchange the ball, both teams fell into a relaxed stance. The quarterback then ran 65 yards down the sidelines for the score.

Intelligent Behavior: Enjoyment of Problem Solving. Many people don't enjoy the challenge of solving problems. They see thinking as hard work and back away from situations that demand too much of it. On the other hand, intelligent human beings get "turned on" by a good problem.

Sports Example: You're a quarterback and your team is behind by six points with a minute left to play in the game. You've got the ball on your own 15-yard line and you need to go 85 yards in 60 seconds. Do you fold under the pressure, or do you thrive under it? Intelligent players enjoy the challenge. Like the Chinese, they recognize that challenge is just another word for "opportunity."

CREATIVITY

Education for creativity is nothing short of education for learning.
                                                    - Erich Fromm

Questions are the creative acts of intelligence.
                                                    - Frank Kingdon

There's one other form of intelligent behavior that we need to talk about, and that is creativity. Intelligent people know how to be creative. They aren't always born creative, but they know how to do things that will help them to be more creative.

Now, what do you think of when you hear someone described as a "creative" person? Do you think of artists? Musicians? Writers? Do you ever think of athletes?

Creativity is the ability to improvise, to experiment, and to think of new things. Basketball is a constant process of improvising, but many players don't do it. They don't experiment. They are rule-bound.

Being a creative athlete is a balancing act. Like a good chef, you have to know the proper ingredients, but be able to deviate from them to create something wonderful. That's what that little Kansas football team did when they pulled the "mother of all quarterback sneaks." Everything they did was within the rules—and completely unexpected.

One of the greatest myths about creativity is that it's a matter of talent. Like intelligence, many people believe you either have it or you don't. But that's not true. Creativity, like other skills, can be developed. How can you do it?

How to Get Your Creative Juices Flowing:

- *Be patient.* In most creative activities, there's a period of time where you're trying to figure how to put things together. Don't get anxious while you wait for the pieces to fall into place. Writers know that the more they worry about how a story will take shape, the less likely they are to finish the story. With basketball, you may find that some new system you're working on just isn't coming together. You can either get frustrated and give up, or you can be patient. Eventually, it will work out.

- *Be willing to keep going.* What makes creative people special is how they face obstacles. It's that "enjoyment of problem solving" that we talked about earlier. If you get dropped to second string, do you use it as an excuse to quit or a reason to persist and solve the problem that is cutting down your playing time?

- *Be willing to grow.* There's something called the "Sophomore Jinx" where a player who is outstanding the first year doesn't do well the second year. This usually happens because players think, "This worked really well for me, so I won't change a thing." So they don't change, but everyone around them does. Suddenly, their game isn't new anymore. If you want to be a creative player, you have to realize you can always improve your game, no matter how good it is or how well it works for you now.

- *Be willing to be uncomfortable.* Let's say you've always played in one position, and now your coach wants to switch you to a different position. Do you gripe and moan about the new position because it "feels funny," or do you use it to develop additional skills and to learn more about the game?

- *Be satisfied by a job well done.* For truly creative people, it's not the awards that matter, it's doing a good job. John Stockton is one of our all-time best NBA point guards, but any sportswriter who has ever struggled to interview him will tell you that Stockton couldn't care less about being famous. In fact, he'd just as soon not be famous—because it gets in the way of his job. For Stockton, satisfaction appears to come from being a good player and helping his team win—not from seeing his name in the paper.

- *Believe in yourself.* There are many times in the lives of almost all creative people when they begin to doubt their ideas and themselves. At such times, you need to believe in yourself even when others don't.

HEAD GAMES

Have you ever lain in bed at night after a game, going over the whole thing in your mind? Basketball player Pete Maravich said that he would mentally replay every game in his head. This kind of mental "game playing" can actually help you improve your basketball skills. It's also a good way to get better at learning just about anything.

All the best athletes are pretty much in top physical condition and possess the same level of athleticism. So if you match up two top athletes whose physical skills are equal, who will win? The athlete who is the better thinker.

Mental rehearsal is one way to improve your basketball thinking and playing skills. What is mental rehearsal? It consists of imagining a motion (or move) or series of motions (or moves) and the situation in which they will be performed. For example, you can use mental rehearsal to improve your free throw performance. You do this by seeing yourself standing at the free throw line holding the ball, hearing the distractions of the crowd. You see the position of your hands on the ball. You see how your arms lift as you begin your shot. You see which way your body leans as the shot leaves your hands.

There is a difference between mental rehearsal and simple imagery. With imagery (which is another mental skill that athletes hear a lot about), you are developing a picture of what you *want* to happen (i.e., you want the ball to go through the net, so that's what you picture happening). With mental rehearsal you:

(1) **Picture what is actually happening**. In this case, you might see yourself leaning away from the ball as you shoot.

(2) **You *analyze* what is happening**. Leaning away from the ball causes it to fall short of the hoop.

(3) **You *correct* what is happening**. You see yourself leaning into the ball instead of away from it.

(4) **You then visualize what you want to happen**—the ball falling through the hoop.

Mentally rehearsing a skill strengthens the connections in the brain that control your performance. You see, every time you perform a skill, tiny electrical circuits are established in the nervous system and in the muscles that perform that skill. When you perform the skill mentally—in other words, when you *imagine* yourself doing it—it sends the same impulses to the brain. This is sometimes called "muscle memory."

USE IT OR LOSE IT

You don't learn anything from a book. When you actually do it, that's when you learn.

- Wendy Guerra, North Hollywood High School student

Learn to Learn

In a book called *Peak Learning*, author Ronald Gross tells a story from *The Wizard of Oz*. In the story, the Scarecrow asks the Wizard for brains. The Wizard tells the Scarecrow that he really doesn't need any brains because he's learning something every day. But the Scarecrow insists. So the Wizard says, "If you will come to me tomorrow morning, I will stuff your head with brains. I cannot tell you how to use them, however; you must find that out for yourself."

Athletes often don't think of themselves as intelligent in the way an A student is thought to be intelligent. However, you are learning things every day without even realizing it. You just have to figure out how to use what you are learning.

Reading this book will not make you into an athlete. If you want to become a better basketball player, you have to go out and use the things you read in this book. You have to *do* them. That is what will make the difference in your performance.

It is the same way with any kind of learning. Remember what we said before? Learning is active. If you want to learn, you have to do.

The Los Angeles Unified School District has been part of a national experiment to improve science and math education. In order to help students learn math and science better, teachers have been spending less time on textbooks and more time on teaching students with lessons from everyday life. "You need to have students engage in real inquiry to have them remember concepts," said Chris Holle, science coordinator of the district's reforms. "Unless you *use* science and math, it won't become a permanent fixture in your mind."

Are you more excited about the idea of learning now? Do you feel more confident about your ability to learn? I hope so. Because now that we've talked about the why's and how's of learning, it's time to talk about the what's.

Chapter  3

LEARN THE FUNDAMENTALS

Some of these young players don't care about fundamentals. They only care about highlight reels.

- George Karl, former coach of the Seattle SuperSonics

You have to know the things fundamentally....like a dancer, you've rehearsed so many times you don't go out and worry about making mistakes.

- Oscar Robertson, NBA Hall-of-Fame Player

Nowadays, young people from peewee leagues through the pros are deficient in basic skills—such as shooting from a jump stop rather than a stride stop, or blocking a shot without swatting it into the stands. The fundamentals situation in basketball is serious. Athletic ability—quickness and vertical jumping ability—have all but replaced technique as far as offensive fundamentals are concerned.

WHAT DO WE MEAN BY "FUNDAMENTAL"?

A player with court sense is a player who first knows the fundamentals of the sport. What do we mean when we say "fundamental"? The fundamentals are the basics. For example, in basketball, they are the essential skills that you need to have in order to be a good player. They include basic motion fundamentals, footwork fundamentals, free throw fundamentals, individual offensive moves, fundamentals of moving without the ball, and post play fundamentals.

WHY IS IT IMPORTANT TO LEARN THE FUNDAMENTALS?

Fundamentals are the key—from youth leagues all the way up to the majors—to playing your best. The player who makes it at any level is the one who works on drills, listens, learns and practices, practices, practices!

- Jim Riggleman, Chicago Cubs manager

Champions in any field have made a habit of doing what others find boring or uncomfortable.

- Anonymous

There are many reasons why learning the fundamentals is so important.

Learning the fundamentals helps you play the game better. If you learn the fundamentals early, you will pick up the game much easier. Don't push the fundamentals aside, thinking you can learn them later. As one sportswriter noted: "The NBA isn't the ideal place for youngsters to develop fundamentals."

Learning the fundamentals gives you confidence. Athletes who master fundamental skills gain a competitor's confidence. If you don't have the fundamentals then it doesn't matter how much you know about the game, because you won't be able to execute. Learning the fundamentals gives you the confidence to be creative.

Learning the fundamentals keeps you from getting hurt. In May of 1989, Jon Peters became the only high school baseball player to land on the cover of *Sports Illustrated*. He had just set a national high school record of 51 straight wins. Peters never went on to pitch in the major leagues, though. Instead, he played off and on in college, and then quit for good just three years after his cover story. The reason? His arm was blown out. "I just had bad mechanics," Peters said.

Randy Johnson, pitcher for the Seattle Mariners, understands what Peters was talking about. At 6'10" tall, with a fastball that measures as fast as 102 MPH, Johnson has become one of the best pitchers in the major leagues. However, there was a time not long ago that he was thinking about quitting baseball. Because he is so tall, Johnson often had trouble coordinating his pitching motion. Sometimes he would strike out a batter, only to walk the next three batters. Then Nolan Ryan, baseball's all-time strikeout king, stepped into the picture.

"He took me aside and helped me with my mechanics," Johnson told a reporter for *People* magazine. "I had a million-dollar arm, but I wasn't thinking enough about how to be a pitcher."

Learning the fundamentals—how to balance yourself, how to position your hands when you shoot—can help you improve your shooting and increase your longevity in the game.

Learning the fundamentals can make up for a lack of athletic ability. Learning the fundamentals can give you an edge over players with better physical skills who maybe aren't willing to work as hard to master the basics. Let's use another baseball example: bunting. It's a fundamental baseball skill, just as shooting is for basketball, but you don't see baseball players putting a lot of effort into working on their bunting skills. One reason, unfortunately, is because most bunts are sacrifice bunts—which means they don't help a player's stats.

Some players, however, see the importance of developing a skill that not everyone has. "I don't have much power, so I have to do things like bunt," says Pittsburgh second baseman Tony Womack. Former major leaguer Rod Carew says, "I worked at it for about an hour every day, because it was a very important part of my game. It seems now guys are mostly thinking about trying to hit the ball into the seats."

A team that is good at the fundamentals will also find that they can do well, even if they don't have an athletic "superstars" on their team. I remember one of the announcers on "Monday Night Football" commenting that one of the reasons the Carolina Panthers expansion team had been so successful in their first season was because they were very fundamentally sound. They didn't make a lot of mistakes in their playing.

Learning the fundamentals is what champions do. Let me tell you a story about the Los Angeles Dodgers. This is a team that has displayed poor fundamentals for most of the last nine years. Fundamentals have cost them games. Fundamentals have cost them championships. Nevertheless, one day in August 1997, the Dodgers did something that was fundamentally beautiful.

In a game against Philadelphia, with a Phillie on first base and no outs, the batter bunted down the third-base line. The Dodger third baseman ran up, fielded the ball, and threw the batter out at first. Meanwhile, the guy on first rounded second and tried to surprise the Dodgers by running to third. But he was met by Dodger catcher Mike Piazza, who made a leaping catch to tag the runner out.

"What's so great about that?" you ask. "Isn't that what the catcher is supposed to do?" Yes, it is! But most catchers—Dodgers or otherwise—don't bother, because the chances of a runner trying to take third base like that are slim. Even Piazza admitted that two years earlier, he probably wouldn't have made that play. But experience as a big league catcher showed him that champions do the things that not everyone is willing to do. Said Mike Scioscia, the Dodger coach who helped Piazza: "I'm starting to see him do the little things it takes to win a championship."

As I mentioned before, John Wooden insisted that each of his basketball players repeatedly practice the fundamentals. While some of the players initially resisted practicing what they already did well, mastery of the fundamentals proved to be one of the difference-makers on the court. Wooden's focus was always on excellence—not winning. The winning just naturally followed.

THERE'S ALWAYS ROOM FOR A KID WHO CAN SHOOT

Kids work on their jams, their garbage moves, anything but shooting. It's a fact. Kids don't shoot the ball anymore. Look around high school and college basketball, how many good shooters are there? I can't wait till I'm a parent because my kid is going to be a shooter. Everybody wants to watch a dunk, but there's always going to be room for a kid who can shoot.

- Mike Anderson, basketball coach, Bolsa Grande, CA

If you're one of the many young players today who has the

mistaken idea that dunking is a fundamental basketball skill, then we should probably review what the fundamentals really are.

There are many basketball fundamentals—both individual fundamentals and game fundamentals. There are also plenty of books and tapes available that can help you learn these fundamentals in-depth. So if you really want to learn a lot about how to shoot better or improve your rebounding, go to the library and find the information there. For the purpose of this book, we will just talk briefly about the fundamental skills that are most important to developing your court sense. These skills include:

- *Shooting*
  - free throws
  - field goals
- *Ball-handling*
  - dribbling
  - passing
  - receiving the ball
- *Passing*
- *Defense*
- *Rebounding*

Shooting:

You should work on three shooting fundamentals—rhythm, mechanics, and balance. The most difficult one to work on is rhythm. Shaquille O'Neal would be a better free-throw shooter if he had better rhythm. His free throws are out of rhythm and his mechanics are poor. Larry Bird is a good example of someone who had rhythm and mechanics. "He [was] a totally fundamental shooter," says shooting expert Tom Marumoto of Newport Beach. "He didn't play basketball until the eighth grade, but he make himself a great shooter by shooting 600 shots a day. As a pro, he did that, too."

These days in the NBA, shots are going in the basket at a rate of 43 percent, the worst shooting percentage in 31 years. The league scoring average is down to 94 points, the lowest since 1954. "I think it's the way the NBA has marketed guys," said Eric Musselman, coach and general manager of the Continental Basketball Association's Florida

Beach Dogs. "They market guys before their games are fully developed, so all you see are the dunks. Jordan is the most fundamentally sound player in the NBA, but all they talk about are his dunks. His flashiness overshadows his ability to shoot the ball."

More and more, it is the girls who are perfecting the art of shooting. Girls are more open to being taught the proper technique. Also, there isn't as much show in the girl's game because they can't get up in the air as high. That means the fundamental part has become extremely important.

Ball-handling:

How well a person handles the ball—dribbles and passes—is what separates the good players from the not-so-good. Although shooting is the first fundamental skill that most players work on, you won't be able to get good shots for yourself or your teammates unless you can get the ball into position—and that requires ball-handling. Ball handling is easily the most neglected fundamental in the game today.

Dribbling:

How do you dribble? Is your head down? Are you constantly looking to make sure you still have the ball?

A good dribbler should be able to keep his head and eyes up at all times, so you can see the court and the other players.

You need to develop a feel for the ball. Just the touch of your fingertips should be enough to control the ball as you dribble. Also, you should use only one hand, wrist, and lower arm to maneuver the ball.

You should be able to dribble equally well with either hand. I remember a particular summer league game the summer before I went off to college. I had just played what I thought was an outstanding game—I had 17 points and a high number of assists. However, a famous coach was in the stands that night and a comment he made got back to me: "Selleck played a good game, but he only goes one way—to his right." After that, I spent the rest of the summer only going to my left with my dribble and drive. It strengthened my game tremendously.

Passing:

Nate "Tiny" Archibald, an NBA All-Star, once said, "To be a good passer you have to realize that one guy's open so you try to pass the ball the best possible way. Whether it's behind your back, a flick of the wrist, over the head pass or whatever, try to have a vision of the whole court."

Passing is about getting the ball to a player in a good position to score. You need to be able to do an accurate, crisp pass that can be received easily.

Before you start working on those behind-the-back passes that look so neat on television, make sure you have mastered the basic ones: the two-handed chest pass, the two-handed bounce pass, the two-handed overhead pass, and the baseball pass. Don't telegraph your passes, try to fake often before you pass, and vary your passes as much as possible to keep your opponent off guard.

Defense:

The dictionary says that a defender is "one who asserts, guards, prohibits, opposes." Bill Russell, my roommate for the college All-Star Game in 1956, says that: "Defense is a matter of pride."

Defense is played in three places: in your heart, on your feet, and in your head. Basically, anyone with the determination to work hard and the desire to play well can be a good defender. That's where the heart comes in.

Next, defense involves good balance. When I teach this, I ask my players to get into a defensive position, then I gently push at their chest and shoulders. They almost always fall backward, because they are off-balance. You need to be standing on the balls of your feet so that you are balanced and ready to move in any direction.

Finally, defense is a head game. First, you need to recognize in your own head how important defense is to winning games. Then you need to find the best ways to defend the opposing player. This involves thinking. For example, what are your opponent's favorite shots? Is your opponent right- or left-handed? In what area does he or she like to get the ball? Which way do they like to turn? Can they use their weak hand? What are his or her favorite moves?

Rebounding:

With rebounding, size is not the most important thing. It's knowing how to use your body, and anticipating where the ball is going when it leaves the shooter's hand. Larry Bird didn't jump the highest, but he was a great rebounder. The good rebounder goes to the spot where the ball will bounce off the rim. This is a skill learned by observing, experiencing, and practicing.

Dennis Rodman, regardless of what anyone thinks about him as a person, is an exceptional player. He is fundamentally sound when it comes to his game—especially rebounding. What does he do? He rebounds up through the ball—meaning he anticipates and has superior timing as opposed to out-jumping his opponents. His positioning is also superb. Most rebounders are about keeping their position. Rodman's positioning is based on the offensive ball movement—where the ball is offensively, first and foremost. First, he picks up the ball, then he picks up his man. Thus, he is a step ahead of most players when it comes to going after the ball.

HOW TO LEARN THE FUNDAMENTALS

To this day, I consider preparation the most enjoyable part of my work, and the most challenging. To the extent my teams have succeeded, I'd say that solid preparation—not talent or strategy—was the primary factor.
- Bill Parcells, NFL coach

If I had six hours to chop down a tree, I'd spend the first four hours sharpening the saw.
- Abraham Lincoln

That which we persist in doing becomes easier for us to do. Not that the nature of the thing itself has changed, but that our ability to do it is increased.
- Ralph Waldo Emerson

A golf pro was approached by two women. "Do you wish to learn to play golf, Ma'am?" he asked one of them.

"Oh, no," she said. "It's my friend who wants to learn. I learned how yesterday."

Fundamentals are about preparation. Preparation is key to success in just about anything you will ever do. Complete preparation is both the most difficult and the most important part of any learning process. If you prepare well, then the actual doing is easy.

For example, one of my favorite places to eat is a little Chinese restaurant where you walk down a row of dishes filled to the brim with finely chopped vegetables and meats of all kinds. You point out which items you want, and the chef stir-fries them together in a matter of seconds. How easy it looks! Of course, once you've spent hours in the preparation, the cooking is easy.

Any obstacles you have ever encountered or may someday encounter in your basketball career are almost always the direct result of insufficient or improper preparation.

Preparation is your foundation. A strong foundation is essential to building anything. A solid foundation based upon preparation is what will help give your career a long life. World-class and professional athletes make it a habit to return to basics and strengthen their foundation, or fundamentals.

And how do they do that? One word: practice.

PRACTICE MAKES PERFECT

What is the difference between sports skills and physical skills? Physical skills are what you were born with—your natural ability. Everyone has different natural abilities. Some people have the ability to jump high. Others have a natural ability for good balance.

Sports skills are different than physical skills. You aren't born with them—you have to learn and develop them. Shooting baskets, dribbling, passing, etc., are all examples of sports skills. They are developed through practice.

There are three stages of practice that you need to go through in order to develop your skills. These are:

Stage One: Learning
This is where you first learn the correct form, footwork, and movements of basketball. There are a lot of stops and starts in stage one practicing, as you constantly make adjustments and corrections.

Stage Two: Mechanical

When you reach the mechanical stage, your performance no longer needs correcting, but you still need to think about it in order to do it right. Your movements are not smooth yet.

Stage Three: Fluid

By this time, the skill has become second nature to you. You can do it without thinking. This leaves your mind free to think about the things that have to do with court sense.

CORRECT PRACTICE MAKES PERFECT

Did you know that you have to learn how to practice, just like anything else? After all, it's not really practice that makes perfect— it's correct practice that makes perfect. If you're not practicing effectively, then you might as well not practice at all. How can you make sure your practices are effective?

(1) **Use proper technique**. The NBA's foul shot percentage has always been between 63 percent and 78 percent. Why? The NBA players have plenty of time to practice, so what's the problem? They lack the fundamentals. Shooting 50 foul shots a day does not improve your shooting—unless you are practicing with the proper technique. *Proper shooting technique is a fundamental that both youth players and professional players need to practice regularly.*

(2) **Begin slowly**. When you begin practicing a new skill, you should always start slowly so you develop the habit of doing it correctly. Practice slowly 100 times (or until you have the correct form mastered). Then practice at half speed 100 times. Finish by practicing at full 100 times.

(3) **Focus on your weak points**. The most effective use of practice time is to focus on fixing weaknesses. The same amount of time devoted to improving strengths will not improve your play that much. With weaknesses, there's more room for improvement. Also, improving a weakness opens up additional strategic options. Stan Albreck

had a short-lived career as a coach, but he was truly a thinking coach. When Albreck took over the Chicago Bulls, Michael Jordan had never been a point guard. He had never had to play with the ball off his dribble. Albreck saw the need for Jordan to acquire this skill, so he had Jordan play point guard so he could learn to play with the ball off his dribble. Michael improved this weakness to the point where he became the greatest point guard ever.

(4) **Take advantage of the off-season**. Players are made in the off-season. This is when you have the opportunity to improve your weaker skills. For example, if you are a shooting guard, work in the off-season on ball-handling so you play point guard—thus increasing your value. One coach was annoyed by his players' inability to dribble with both hands. "Can anybody here honestly tell me they worked on their weak hand?" he asked. "Anybody? Too busy trying to dunk— trying to dribble between your legs, tryin' all this fancy ****. *Work on your weak hand!* That's what summers are for. The weak hand! The weak hand! You need to put your body between your opponent and the ball. You've got to be able to use both hands. That's the difference between a mediocre player and a good player..."

(5) **Practice fundamentals, not flash**. Clem Haskins, coach of the Minnesota Golden Gophers, will not allow any dunking for the first three weeks of practice, so players—especially new kids from high school or community college—will be forced to work on the fundamentals instead of relying solely on their athleticism.

One reason Arizona won the NCAA championship game in 1997 was because it did what no one else does anymore: It made free throws—34 of 41. Arizona showed solid fundamentals.

PRACTICING A LOT MAKES EVEN MORE PERFECT

Until one man makes every shot or one man stops every shot, you have to work to get better.

- Olivier Saint-Jean, Sacramento Kings rookie

Tony Gwynn of the San Diego Padres once said: "Baseball is a lot more than nine innings. That's all people see and that's a lesson everybody has to learn. Some of these guys have to mature and understand what it takes to be successful in this game." Gwynn knows what it takes to be successful. He gets to the park early, takes extra batting practice, and studies film after games.

Peter Vidmar, who won an Olympic gold medal in gymnastics, is another example of how extra practice can pay off. Vidmar said that two or three years before the Olympics, he realized he was only as good as his teammates and his opponents. But he needed to be better if he was going to win the gold. So he decided he would go to practice 15 minutes earlier than any teammate and leave 15 minutes later than anyone else. That doesn't sound like much, but it added up to 52 extra "practice days" a year. Those 52 extra practices are what helped Peter Vidmar to win a gold medal. Just an extra 15 minutes before and 15 minutes after.

During the 1987 NBA season, Larry Bird, Danny Ainge, and Magic Johnson all shot 90 percent or better from the free-throw line. They were also the only players who were willing to practice at least 100 free throws per day. Their two teams were also the ones who played for the NBA Championship that year. Coincidence? You tell me.

As a senior, Jackie Styles was described as the best high school player in Kansas and one of the best players in the nation. She averaged 44 points a game and set the state's all-time scoring record. She also holds the state record for the most points in a game with 71. Her talent comes from constant practice. She begins the day with a shoot-around. After school is team practice. After practice, she continues the workout alone. Two or three times a week, her workout includes a routine of hitting 1,000 shots, which can take as long as four hours.

PLAY IT AGAIN, SAM

The biggest complaint about practice is that it's boring. People get tired of doing the same thing over and over again. Nevertheless, if you want to improve as a player, you have to work at it.

Maybe it will help to know why it's important to repeatedly practice the same thing. First of all, by doing something repeatedly, you improve your level of consistency. Coaches don't always take enough time to work on this, so you might have to assume the responsibility yourself.

Second, what you don't do in practice, you won't do in games. Why? Because of habit. If it's not what you're used to doing, you won't do it. So you have to practice something long enough to make it a habit. When you develop good habits through repetition, then you don't have to think about them during the game. That frees you to make good decisions.

Finally, repetitive practice is what allows a team to work together smoothly. A basketball team should work together like the fingers on a hand. That kind of coordinated movement takes months to achieve—and some teams never achieve it.

Chapter 4

LEARN TO BE CONFIDENT

Sometimes quarterbacks, despite their obvious physical tools, just don't have it. Football players in the NFL smell a quarterback's lack of confidence the way a dog smells fear.

- Tim Green, former NFL player

The minute you start talking about what you're going to do if you lose, you've lost.

- George Shultz, former Secretary of State

Confidence. It's often talked about, but rarely understood. For many, it comes and goes. One day you have lots of it; the next day you have none. Confidence is not something you are born with or can buy. But it can be developed, and you have the power to do it.

WHAT IS CONFIDENCE?

It's not about making a lot of adjustments right now. It's about believing in what we're doing.

- Karl Malone, before Game 3 of the 1997 NBA Finals
(after losing to Chicago, 2-0)

Lots of people have the wrong idea about confidence. They think that confidence is something they either have or they don't. Sometimes athletes think confidence is something that descends on them like a revelation from heaven, as a reward for good performance. Well, guess what? Confidence isn't something you're given. You control it.

Confidence is what you think about yourself and your game. Confidence is an inner feeling or sense of who you are and how you are capable of performing. It's not tied to winning or outcome. It's knowing that you will play to your capability. It's a positive attitude. It's a sense of respect for yourself and others.

If you are a confident player, you have faith in your ability. Competition doesn't worry you, it excites you. Winning or losing is not as important as playing your best. When you lose, you don't think thoughts like: "That team really screwed us over," or "Losing is so embarrassing!" Instead, you think: "Wow! Those guys must have been really good to have beaten us!"

If you are a confident player, you don't need to be a braggart. That's because confident players like to focus on the future, not their past accomplishments.

Confident players don't care what others think of them. They are self-oriented, not other-oriented.

Sometimes people think this means you're cold or stuck-up. Allen Iverson, the NBA's 1997 Rookie of the Year, has certainly developed a reputation for confidence that isn't always positive. Derrick Coleman, one of Allen Iverson's teammates, said, "I don't think he pays attention to what people say. You've got to be like that."

Little kids are sometimes our greatest examples of confidence, especially when they're still young enough to not worry about making a good impression on others. Tom Crum, who has worked a lot with young people teaching martial arts, says that when he works with little kids, he never asks for volunteers because everyone will stand up. They haven't learned yet to be afraid of looking silly. When he works with high school kids, he picks volunteers ahead of time, because everyone's worried about not looking good.

Confident athletes continually strive to be the best they can be. That's why we hear about athletes who tolerate long periods of hard work, adversity, or even failure because of the belief that one day they will be one of the best. Tim Hardaway endured a blown knee, being thrown away by the Golden State Warriors, and a period of free agency when everyone was looking for someone like Gary Payton or Chris Childs. Pat Riley didn't particularly want him, but took him anyway. Hardaway went on to lead the Miami Heat to the NBA playoffs. "He's a very, very courageous player," Riley said. "He looks fear right in the eye, and says, 'Get the **** out of my way. I got something to do.'"

Does being confident mean not being nervous? No, you can be confident and be nervous. It's called good nervousness. Good nervousness makes you perform better. Bad nervousness hurts your performance. Tom Lehman, one of professional golf's top players, said that he loves to "feel the nerves from being in the hunt." That is positive nervousness. It's connected to the body's release of adrenaline—the 'fight or flight' response that our body makes to protect us.

Is every athlete who projects confidence really confident? Not necessarily. Some athletes are merely pseudo-confident. Pseudo means "fake" or "pretend." You've probably known someone who is pseudo-confident. They have talent, but they're not certain about it. They seem tough on the outside, but they're shaky on the inside.

Pseudo-confident athletes tend to brag or exaggerate their skills. What other people think matters a lot to them. That's why they often take on opponents who are bigger or tougher than they are—so that they will look good in front of others. Another thing pseudo-confident athletes sometimes do is take less talented opponents too lightly—then they end up losing.

Belief in yourself is an essential ingredient for success of any kind. If you believe in yourself, you can accomplish almost everything you desire—provided you develop your skills.

Coaches, athletes, and sports psychologists agree that self-confidence is key to consistently high performance. Self-confidence leads to being more relaxed, less anxious, and not as easily intimidated. Self-confidence and court sense are closely related—when you have self-confidence, it is easier to develop your court sense. Without self-confidence, you won't have the faith you need to make good decisions on the court.

HOW CONFIDENT ARE YOU?

How's your confidence level? Low? High? Somewhere in the middle? If any of the following statements describe you as an athlete, then you need to work on your confidence.

- You struggle constantly for external recognition rather than internal satisfaction. For example, you'd rather play a bad game and win instead of play a good game and lose.

• You measure your self-worth on the basis of each performance. If you play well, you feel like a good person. If you play poorly, you feel like a loser.

• You focus on perfection rather than excellence. People who think they need to be perfect can never win—because no one's perfect. You can be excellent, however.

• You beat yourself up when you make mistakes, instead of using them as an opportunity for learning.

• You blame others or your circumstances when things go wrong. ("The refs were out to get us!" "Their floor was really lousy!") This leaves you feeling out of control.

• You have unrealistic goals that result in frustration, disappointment, and distraction.

HOW CAN YOU IMPROVE YOUR CONFIDENCE?

A friend of mine told me a story about an extremely talented high school tennis player whom he was counseling. The girl had been number two as a freshman and number one as a sophomore. Now, as a junior, she and everyone else expected that she would win the league championship. She came to my friend looking for the confidence to do so. He told her that confidence came in tiny green pills that cost a dollar each. She laughed and said, "I'll take two dozen."

The point of this story is, you don't develop confidence instantly. It's a continual process of growth and development that involves working on such things as your ability to master the basketball fundamentals, prepare well, be mentally tough, and take risks.

Learn to Be Confident

CONFIDENCE AND THE FUNDAMENTALS

Charles O'Bannon's crowning moment came with less than two minutes to play, the shot clock ticking down below five, the crowd roaring, and the Bruins up by a single point, 79-78.

Starting with a slow dribble at the top of the key, with Donald Watts slapping at the ball, O'Bannon took two steps to the right, then suddenly launched himself spinning left, stopped himself in the lane, and buried a wide-open six-footer against a stunned Husky defense to give UCLA an 81-78 lead.

"I work on that every day in practice," O'Bannon said. "I had confidence—that's the bottom line."

- from the *Los Angeles Times*

Confidence is what comes after you have learned the skills, practiced them diligently, and can now perform them.

Learning the fundamentals helps you gain confidence. That's why we talked about fundamentals first. They're the foundation upon which everything else is built.

I have heard many parents say over the years: "Can you help my son (or daughter)? All they lack is confidence." Perhaps these parents should take a deeper look at the issue. What their kids really need help with are their skills. It's not confidence they should be looking for—it's ability. With the ability, the confidence will come.

Confidence comes from competence, which means knowing that you can do something successfully. Competence is mastering a skill. I have always chuckled on the inside whenever someone said I was a natural athlete. There was nothing natural about it! I prepared. In elementary school, I would shoot basket after basket in my backyard before making the four-mile walk to school. I'd set up chairs in the gym and practice dribbling between them—sometimes blindfolded. It was the hours of practice, passing against the wall if there wasn't anyone else to play with, that gave me the confidence to try it in a game.

There's an old saying, "Familiarity breeds contempt." I would also like to say that "Familiarity breeds confidence." If you've never done something before, it's doubtful that you will be confident at it. For example, not long ago I was a volunteer at a middle school Sports Day in San Diego. Because of the large number of kids, they gave each kid a four-digit number, and abbreviated their school name to just two letters (for example, "RO" for Roosevelt). My job was to record the long jump distances. Each participant had three jumps. I almost panicked at the thought of having to remember all those letters and numbers. My confidence in my ability was pretty low. However, once I got the hang of it, or increased my familiarity with the job, my confidence rose and I did just fine.

So learn the fundamentals. If you learn the correct way to play basketball or any sport, you will always have that set of fundamentals to fall back on. If your game starts to fall apart, you know what to do to put it back on track and restore your confidence.

CONFIDENCE AND PREPARATION

One important key to success is self-confidence. An important key to self-confidence is preparation. Complete mental and physical preparation has to do with sacrifice and self-discipline. And that comes from within. Start by setting modest goals which are meaningful, but obtainable. For example, every Sunday night write down four things that you want to accomplish for the following week, and then make sure that seven days later when you make up your next list, all four items have been crossed off. These small but meaningful completed tasks should generate much self-confidence as times goes by.

- Arthur Ashe, former professional tennis player

Confidence comes from working hard in practice and being focused out there. When you go into a game knowing that you gave it your all, that you prepared as well as you could, your confidence is naturally going to be there.

- Kobe Byrant, Los Angeles Lakers swingman

We talked about preparation when we talked about the importance of learning the fundamentals. To show you just how important preparation is, we're going to talk about it again.

Now, if I say to you, "You need to do a lot of preparation in order to play good basketball," you probably think I'm talking about practice. And that's certainly part of it. But there's more to preparation than shooting a hundred hoops every day.

Setting goals is one of the most important things you can do to help you prepare better. I started setting goals when I was seven or eight. I would spend hours playing imaginary basketball games on the playground, carefully recording the number of shots it took to reach 50 points and victory for my team.

Goals keep you focused on what's important. They help you make good decisions. They help you take control of your life. In my book, *How to Play the Game of Your Life*, I list several tips to help you be better at setting and achieving your goals. These include:

- *Write down your goals.* When you take the trouble to write something down, you're more likely to take the trouble to achieve it.

- *Make your goals positive.* A positive goal is when you say, "I want to increase my free-throw shooting percentage to 80%." You're saying what you want to do. A negative goal is when you say what you don't want to do: "I never want to eat junk food again" is negative. "I will eat more healthy food" is positive.

- *Make your goals measurable.* If your goal is simply to improve your shooting, how will you know when you've done that unless you tell how you will measure your improvement?

Setting goals is just one way of preparing yourself to be a better player. Preparation also includes such things as studying other teams and players and taking good care of yourself physically (that means eating well and getting lots of sleep). There's a scripture in the Bible that says, "If ye are prepared, ye shall not fear." When you prepare yourself by practicing and doing the other things you need to do, it will pay off with confidence on the court.

CONFIDENCE AND MENTAL TOUGHNESS

I have the physical skills to play at the highest level. The reason I haven't succeeded is that I'm not there mentally ... I pray for poise and confidence because I believe that when I'm poised and confident, I can't be stopped.
> \- Trent Dilfer, quarterback for the Tampa Bay Buccaneers

At the professional level, everyone has ability, but some players don't have the mental toughness it takes to be a successful player. Players with court sense are mentally tough. What do you need to do in order to be mentally tough?

(1) **Love the game**. Win or lose, practicing or playing—you have to love what you're doing. Philosopher Alan Watts once said, "You don't sing to get to the end of the song." The same applies to basketball. You don't play just to win—you play because you love to play. If you only play for the trophies or awards, then you will just build up your tension and anxiety, which will make you perform worse.

(2) **Hang tough**. There are talented players who miss a game because of a hangnail. There are less talented players who play through colds, flu, cracked ribs—you name it. Toughness is a crucial element of confidence.

(3) **Keep your cool**. On the court or off, your emotional state of mind affects your confidence. Learn to keep your life in balance and your emotions in check. Don't worry about things that are beyond your control.

(4) **Think positive**. Confident basketball players usually have positive thoughts, positive self-talk, positive images, and positive dreams. They focus on how to accomplish something rather than seeing the barriers in their way. Confident players consistently see themselves winning and being successful. The key is that they have enabling thoughts rather than disabling thoughts. You need to learn to monitor your thinking. If an idea springs into your head, ask yourself:

"Is this idea more likely to help me or hurt me in my effort to become more confident?"

(5) **Never stop trying to improve**. No matter how good you are, you can always be better.

(6) **Remember that confidence is an ongoing battle**. In 1994, Steffi Graf became the first defending champion in history to lose in the first round at Wimbledon. Being good doesn't mean you'll never lose confidence.

CONFIDENCE AND TAKING RISKS

If you want to increase your success rate, double your failure rate.
- Thomas Watson, Sr., founder of IBM

Let me tell you one of my favorite stories. It seems that a young vice president of IBM made a mistake that cost the company $10 million. Since the loss happened back in the days when $10 million was considered to be a lot of money, the president of IBM invited the young man into his office to discuss the situation. The associate quickly said, "I suppose you want my resignation." Mr. Watson replied, "You must be kidding—we have $10 million invested in your education!"

Thomas Watson understood three important principles:

(1) You don't succeed without taking risks.

(2) The more risks you take, the more failures you will probably have.

(3) Every mistake or failure is an opportunity to learn.

Thomas Edison would never have succeeded in creating the light bulb if he had been sidetracked by the thousands of failures he experienced during its development. Instead, each "failure" provided important feedback that drew him closer to a successful result.

Colonel Harland Sanders experienced over one thousand rejections for his now-famous chicken recipe.

The cleansing product Formula 409 had—you've got it—408 unsuccessful attempts before the final product was developed.

Everyone fails. The question is not did you ever or will you ever fail, but can you pick yourself up and move ahead? Failure is an integral part of learning, and court sense is about learning to play the game at a higher level.

When it comes to making mistakes or failing at something, most of us are too hard on ourselves. As I watch my grandson toddling around the house, I think that if he was as hard on himself as most adults are, he might never have learned to walk or talk. I can't imagine little Christian falling down and saying, "Darn! Screwed up again!" Fortunately, he is free of self-criticism. He treats failure the same as success, by just continuing to practice.

In almost all sports, when a player makes a mistake, there is a choice to be made. Do I compound the mistake, or correct it? If your mistake freezes you or throws you off, then you compound it. A block or a "kill" in volleyball isn't a point lost until you stand there, frustrated, and fail to make the best response to keep the ball alive. Oleg Suzdeleff, who was a senior when I was a young basketball player, would pound his fist into the palm of his hand when he would make a mistake. Poom! One pound and that was it—it was on to the next play. When you make a mistake, move on. Get on with the game and help your teammates to do the same. This is the intelligent thing to do. Any lapse of effort, temper, or concentration due to a missed shot, bad pass, or a referee's call, is not only costly to your team, it demonstrates a lack of intelligence and foresight on your part.

John Daly has had considerable ups and downs in his professional golf career, including alcoholism and relationship problems. He said that one of the biggest problems throughout his life has been a lack of self-respect. "I've had a problem forgiving myself for the things I've done." Learning to forgive and forget has improved his golf game.

Coming back to face the 1997-98 season after a couple of close losses to Chicago in the NBA Finals, Utah Jazz coach Jerry Sloan said he was confident the Jazz could go 82-0. When asked if he had done much thinking about those two games the Jazz almost won, Sloan said he never looked back on that kind of stuff.

Confidence involves taking risks, being willing to make mistakes, and knowing how to move on. This doesn't mean that confident players enjoy making mistakes—no one does! But they don't let their mistakes get in the way of where they're going.

CONFIDENCE AND LEARNING

If you're like I was, you probably find it easier to be confident on the court than in the classroom. When I was on the court, I always wanted the ball. It's not because I was a ball hog. It's just that I had the confidence that I could make the pass, or penetrate the defense, or sink the jump shot.

The classroom, however, was a different story. There, I lacked the confidence that I felt on the court. Granted, I always got good grades— but I sweated over every assignment and every test. Whenever I had a paper to write, I always felt that I needed to find out how someone else expressed the idea first. I simply did not trust my own intellectual skills. Unlike when I was on the court, I was afraid to take the risk and possibly fail.

CHOOSE TO BE CONFIDENT

Again, the things that separate the great players from the almost-great have little to do with physical talent. The whole is greater than the sum of its parts because of the way great players think. Their attitudes and beliefs shape their careers as much or sometimes more than their physical talents. Champions choose to be confident. Most of us need to have good results before we can feel confident. Great players are confident even before they start shooting, and stay confident even if they're shooting poorly. You don't have any control over the outcome of any shot after it leaves your hand. But you do have a choice about what happens after the shot. Choose to be confident, and to do those things that will increase your confidence. By doing so, you will be on your way to becoming an intelligent player on and off the court.

Chapter  5

LEARN TO THINK THE GAME

Each game is like a class—I learn something new, either about myself, my teammates or my competition. But it's always something.

- Tim Duncan, San Antonio Spurs

I've played with teams that have championship players on it, legendary guys. Really, at this point, this team isn't [there] yet. Larry and Kevin McHale and Robert Parrish, those guys knew how to prepare themselves for a game. They took care of the little things. They prepared for games by watching films. That type of thing. The things championship teams do.

- Robert Horry, Los Angeles Lakers

WHAT DOES IT MEAN TO "THINK THE GAME"?

Thinking the game means being able to react or respond spontaneously on the court, better and more quickly than your opponents or teammates. Thinking the game involves strategy. Even more, it involves learning every aspect of the game—from the rules of the game to the personalities of the players.

The key to becoming someone who is "basketball smart" doesn't lie in how high your IQ is or how well your brain works. The key is having the willingness, or the desire, to learn. You must have the desire to absorb knowledge of the game from any and every source— your coach, your teammates, the fans...anyone who knows about the game. You have to be willing to read books and articles, attend camps and clinics, and watch games in person and on television. Then you have to follow up by analyzing and discussing the things you've learned with knowledgeable people.

You could say that thinking the game means learning how to think like a coach. Just ask Josh Pastner. Even though he was a member of the University of Arizona's 1996 NCAA championship basketball team, Pastner's goal isn't to become an NBA player. He wants to become a coach. At age 12, he started his intense study of the game. He began calling college coaches to ask for game tapes. He watched game films, studied them, broke them down. He went to lectures on basketball, and read armloads of books on the subject.

Josh used his knowledge of the game to help his teammates win the championship. Said Final Four MVP Miles Simon: "Every night he'd get us back into the gym an extra hour or two to work on shooting. Basically, he would tell me to use my legs and follow through. He worked on the fundamentals."

Added Pac-10 Freshman of the Year Mike Bibby: "When I came here, I don't think I really knew how to shoot. He worked on that category of my game. He told me to snap my wrist, not go backwards."

Arizona's basketball coach Lute Olsen said that Josh made a habit of coming in when assistant coach Jim Rosborough was breaking down tapes of other teams. "Josh wants to understand every nuance."

What are some things you can do to help your understanding of the game?

REACT QUICKLY

According to Pete Newell, a Hall-of-Fame coach who runs a big-man camp for college and professional players, today's players don't read and respond. Instead, they are predisposed to what they are going to do. In other words, their minds are made up. They are hardwired instead of bread boarded. (When designing a software package you put pins and wires on a breadboard and try different connections until you make the right connection. Then you hardwire it, or make it permanent.)

Newell has players at his camps run the following drill to overcome their habit of predetermining what they are going to do. A player has the ball. Newell stands behind the player with the ball and signals the defensive player what to do, so that the ballhandler faces different challenges and has to learn to react quickly to them. It's not an easy thing to do. All of us—athletes included—get "mentally lazy" sometimes. We like to take the path of least resistance. In day-to-day life, mental laziness can result in things like poor grades. But on the court, the penalty of not reacting quickly to changes can be as severe as defeat or serious injury.

Speaking of his days as a coach, Pete Newell says, "We did it all in practice. I wanted my players to recognize and respond on the court instead of having to call a time-out. I didn't even like to call time-outs. I expected my players to respond to the defense instead of me having to do it for them. I never over-coached from the sidelines. We prepared them in practice and let them play. We didn't want to make them dependent on us."

Pete gives an example of a time when his team (California) showed their ability to think the game. They were tied with Oregon State in a regional playoff game to determine who would go the NCAA's. Oregon State had two 7-foot players. Newell's tallest was 6'6." One of the 7-footers was being guarded by a 6'2" player. Newell's team had one day to practice—the game was on Monday night following Friday and Saturday games, and Newell's team had to travel on Sunday.

Oregon State quickly jumped ahead 12-4 in the opening minutes. Newell's team was having trouble with State's two-man game. "All of a sudden, we shifted our defense and rotated to give help underneath," Pete explains. "We did it without a time-out. We won by 18—a great adjustment." After the game, the sportswriters were praising Newell for turning the game around in a matter of minutes with a well-timed adjustment. What did you do, they asked? Newell responded: "You'll have to wait until the players are out of the showers and ask them."

Thinking the game means being able to quickly adapt to situations. Eighty percent of the time you are running a play with options. Twenty percent of the time the play is broken, either by defensive action or the offense's failure to execute. Therefore, you have to adapt to what other people are doing.

SEE THE COURT

Thinking the game involves learning to see the action on the court unfold clearly, almost as if it were in slow motion. This only happens with experience. One young basketball player described the experience like this: "I remember having the sensation that I was on a merry-go-round. The scene was a blur of action. Multi-colored shirts seemed to be rotating around the court and there seemed to be defenders everywhere I looked. Dozens of them at least! Through most of the game my biggest worry was that I would get a pass and dribble to the wrong basket. I kept reminding myself which basket was ours. Ten years later it never occurred to me to think about which basket was ours. If the other team had only four players back on defense, the imbalance would be as obvious as the sofa suddenly missing from your living room. By then, it didn't take counting, but it sure didn't start out that way."

One football player described the frustration of playing against Joe Montana, who had an uncanny ability to see the field: "He could read defenses so well, you felt foolish lining up in some disguised coverage. When he took the snap, he seemed to see so clearly what we were doing that it felt just plain stupid to line up away from the positions we needed to be in. We never seemed to fool him at all. It was like he would drop back smiling at us, knowing immediately that we were already scrambling to recover into our designed coverage. Most quarterbacks would get confused and feel rushed by our disguises, but Montana just seemed to be out there playing the game in slow-motion, seeing everything we were doing before we even had a chance to do it."

Naturally, seeing the court is easier if you're blessed with good peripheral vision. However, the key to getting the big picture is being able to size up the situation quickly and knowing how to react. That is not something you're born with. It's something you learn.

THINK AHEAD

In his memoirs, basketball great Bill Russell shares some thoughts about thinking the game. He noted that he always tried to have two or three moves in mind in advance—such planning cut down on his mental hesitation on the floor and reduced his number of mistakes.

However, as Russell noted, his thinking was not always highly regarded by his teammates:

> The prevailing strategy was that you went out, took your shots and waited to see what happened. It was not considered a game for thinkers. K.C. [Jones] and I were thought to be freaks because of

our dialogues on strategy, which were fun for us but dull to every-one else....We shared an extra fascination for the game because of the mental tinkering we did with it in our bull sessions. For ex-ample, K.C. was instantly aware of what I thought was the best single play I ever made in college. We were playing Stanford in the San Francisco Cow Palace, and one of their players stole the ball at half court for a breakaway lay-up. He was so far ahead of us that no-body on our team bothered to chase him except me. As he went loping down the right side of the court, I left the center position near our basket and ran after him as fast as I could. The guy's lead was so big that he wasn't hurrying. When I reached half court I was flying, but I took one long stride off the left to change my angle, then went straight for the bucket. When the guy went up for his lay-up in the lane, I too went up from the top of the key. I was flying. He lofted the ball up so lazily that I was able to slap it into the backboard before it started down. The ball bounced back to K.C., trailing the play.

Probably nobody in that Cow Palace crowd knew anything about how that play developed. They didn't see where I came from, and they saw only the end of the play. But to K.C. and me, the sweet-ness of the play was the giant step I took to the left as I was building up speed. Without that step the play would have failed, because I'd have fouled the guy by landing on him after the shot. The step to the left gave me just enough angle coming across to miss him and land to the right of him without a foul.

You know, the funny thing about this story is that I'm the guy Bill Russell is talking about. Perhaps as many as two dozen people have asked me about this story over the years. Of course, my recollection of the event is a little different. Everything Russell said was accurate except at the end of the play he did come down on top of me. But everyone (including the refs) were so caught up in watching his dash down court that they failed to notice the foul. Nevertheless, what Russell did was a great example of thinking ahead.*

*Isn't it ironic that Bill Russell's best single play in college was at my expense and mine was at his! Even more remarkable is that both plays are classic examples of court sense. However, Russell's could not have succeeded without his magnificent athleticism (and my body as his cushion).

Learn to Think the Game

KNOW WHAT'S GOING ON

Thinking the game means knowing what's going on—knowing how much time is on the game clock and the shot clock. Knowing when to call time-out. Knowing how to play with three fouls. Knowing when to foul another player. Knowing which player to foul.

Most players assume that what you do in practice will transfer to the game. Unfortunately, practices concentrate primarily on improving physical skills—not mental skills, or, in other words, rapid decision-making. For example, one night I was watching two college teams playing for a bid to the NCAA's. There was less than a minute to play, with one point separating the two teams. The 7'1" center had a good idea, which was to jump out to contain a player coming off a screen with the ball in the mid-court area. However, instead of holding his position (which would have been disruptive to the offense), the center reached out for the ball and got called for a foul. As the players moved to the foul line, you could read the center's lips: "Stupid! Stupid!" He knew that he had not made a smart play. He started to—but he ruined it by not thinking about what he was doing. If he had thought about it, he would have realized that 1) it was absolutely critical not to make any fouls at this point, and 2) reaching usually creates a foul.

Thinking the game means knowing what to do in various situations. For example:

• **Fouls**.

You foul out on the first or second foul—never on the fifth or sixth. Players think that they have five fouls (school) or six fouls (pros) and thus tend not to get serious about fouls until they've committed at least two. So at least one or two of the fouls are unnecessary. Don't foul when you are ahead by three points with seven seconds left or by five points with four minutes left.

• **Leaving the floor**.

Don't let your feet leave the floor without a good reason—such as going up for a shot or rebound. Once you are in the air you have committed yourself, dramatically decreasing your options. So when driving to the basket, don't leave the ground prematurely. On defense, don't run and leap to block a shot or a pass. Instead, approach the player with the ball using short, choppy steps with your feet on the ground so that you can respond to whatever the offensive player might do.

• Good shot or bad shot?

Bad shots lose games. What is a bad shot? A low percentage shot instead of a high percentage shot. A good team is often characterized as taking good shots. They pass up bad shots and wait for better ones. Learn the difference between a 45 percent shot and a 60 percent shot. Basketball is a percentage game. You get X amount of shots on an average per game. When you improve your shot percentage, you improve your chances of winning.

• Defensive fakes.

You don't see much of this. Defensive faking is an attempt to make something happen—to create while on defense when your man has the ball. You fake at him to try to get him to commit himself too soon. For example, you may lunge at him to create the impression you're attacking the ball, or you may fake with your hands to give him the feeling that you are too close—then when he drives for the basket you are ready since you know you have set the trap by acting in an overly aggressive manner.

• When you don't have the ball.

We've already talked about the importance of being able to play without the ball. Let me mention one other thing you should be doing when you don't have the ball: talking. Talking to your teammates can help you and them perform better. Less experienced players might not feel like talking is really all that necessary ("That screen was obvious. Why should I tell him about it?"). But what is obvious to you might not be obvious to your teammate. Talking ("I've got him!") can clear up confusion and prevent players from hesitating to make a move.

• When the clock is stopped.

This is a time of choice—to rest, complain, look at the crowd, whatever. But if you are thinking the game, this is your time to:

- verify how many time-outs are left, how many fouls you
  have to give, and which opponents are in foul trouble
- remind a teammate to drive their man into the screens that
  are available to him
- encourage your teammates
- remind a teammate to block out the free throw shooter
- remind the inbound passer to get the ball
- make suggestions to teammates concerning offense or
  defense
- coach yourself

• **When you are on the bench.**

Just because your body's not on the floor, doesn't mean your head can't be out there. Whether you are a starter or a reserve, take advantage of your time on the bench to study what's going on in the game. What you observe can be invaluable to yourself, your coach, or a teammate. Remember, even coaches don't always know what is going on. One coaching friend of mine likes to have his reserve players keep track of the other team's fouls and remaining time-outs as well as those of his own team. That way they keep their heads in the game, and they can help the coach know when to object if the official makes a correctable error.

KNOW THE RULES

There is a reason for knowing the rules. The obvious reason, of course, is so that you don't break them. But there's another reason. You should know the rules thoroughly so that you can use them to your advantage.

Using the rules creatively to gain an advantage is an art. One of my favorite examples of this kind of creativity comes from the book *Everyone's a Coach*, by Don Shula and Ken Blanchard. In the book, Shula tells the story of Dan Marino's fake grounding of the ball in the last 38 seconds of a game against the New York Jets in 1994:

It looked like improvising, but it was something we started to work into our two-minute drill that year. Bernie Kosar, the quarterback we picked up from Dallas to be our insurance policy for Marino, had experimented with the play at Cleveland and also at Dallas. To pull the play off, the situation had to be just right—a time when the other team would be expecting the quarterback to try to stop the clock by throwing the ball to the ground (that is, legally grounding the ball). When our quarterback is going to ground the ball intentionally, he yells to the team, "Clock! Clock! Clock!" This signals everyone to line up to protect him while he throws the ball to the ground. This in turn stops the clock so we can get into the huddle and call the next play.

In this game against the Jets, it was the ideal situation: 38 seconds to play, and we still had one time-out left. Bernie's on the headset with Dan and sends in the word. Dan yells, "Clock! Clock! Clock!" and the linemen get ready to block. Dan makes eye contact with Ingram, the receiver on the right side. Dan takes the snap, calmly steps back, looks at the ground, and fires the winning touchdown pass to Ingram as the Jets stand there flat-footed, anticipating the stopping of the clock. It couldn't have worked better.

Of course, sometimes using the rules creatively means knowing when to break the rules. In the 1976 NBA finals, the Boston Celtics were playing the Phoenix Suns. The Celtics were ahead with fewer than 10 seconds to play, and the Suns' star point guard, Paul Westphal, was on the bench. Phoenix was out of time-outs, and Westphal knew it. Still, he told the head coach, Cotton Fitzsimmons, to call one anyway. It took Fitzsimmons a few seconds to figure out what Westphal was thinking. Then he realized that if Phoenix called a timeout, Boston would gain possession after a single free-throw attempt and have to inbound the ball, which Phoenix might be able to intercept. Even if Boston made its free throw (which they did), they would only have a two-point lead. If Phoenix could gain possession on the inbound pass and score, it might force the game into overtime.

That's exactly what happened. Unfortunately (for Phoenix), Boston won in overtime, but the strategy gave Phoenix a second chance that they otherwise might not have had. Is it any wonder that Paul

Westphal went on to become a coach himself? Even when he wasn't in the game physically, he was in it mentally. That is one of the characteristics that distinguishes the superstars from players with equal or greater athletic talent.

KNOW YOUR ENVIRONMENT

All gymnasiums are not created equal. Some are cavernous; others resemble cracker boxes. Some have acoustics that make a sonic boom sound quiet. Some have baskets that are in place while others have mobile baskets that can be moved on and off the floor. Still other gyms have baskets that retract and must be lowered before the game. These variations can be important because they influence the amount of playing area under and around the basket. They also can create barriers that affect your moves when driving in for a layup.

What are some other things you should notice about your playing environment?

- Notice how tight or loose the rims are in an opponent's gym. The tighter the rim, the more likely a missed shot off the rim will carom to a guard outside who may be able to score on a fastbreak.

- Notice where the dead spots are on your own floor and on an opponent's floor so you can either avoid them or force an opponent to dribble over one.

- Notice the distance between the in-bound line and the crowd; the shorter it is, the more crowd noise and distraction and the more important it is to be able to run the baseline when you inbound.

- Notice what kind of floor you're playing on. Some gyms have concrete subfloors under the hardwood instead of a more giving support structure. (If you are trying to decide between several colleges, you should carefully consider this factor before making a decision; it could affect your physical well-being and longevity in the game.)

All of these differences and many others give the player with keen court sense endless opportunities to turn the game to the advantage of his or her team. How often did the Boston Celtics cause an opposing player to turn the ball over by forcing him to dribble over dead spots on the old Boston Gardens parquet floor? The Celtics knew where those spots were and avoided them, but few players on other teams could claim they never fell victim to one of Boston's "floor leprechauns."

KNOW THE PLAYERS, COACHES, AND OFFICIALS

Know your opponents. You should know the strengths and weaknesses of each opponent (starting with whether a player is right-handed or left-handed or both). You should also be aware of your opponent's limitations in any given game—such as having several fouls early on or favoring one leg over another because of an injury. Knowing an opponent's shooting strengths gives you an opportunity to deny particular shots. Deliberately fouling a weak free-throw shooter versus a strong one is another no-brainer, but one that even professionals can mess up in the heat of a game.

Know your teammates. If you have the ball in a three-on-two fastbreak, will you pass it to the teammate who is erratic on lay-ups or the one who consistently ices them? The answer may seem obvious, but it may depend on which hand will be used to lay the ball in the bucket. If you don't know your teammates' strengths, you may make the wrong choice.

Know your coach. Some coaches are like human volcanoes, pacing the sidelines and just waiting for an opportunity to erupt. Others control their emotions during a game. Some coaches welcome player input; others won't tolerate it. A player with good court sense understands and uses the coach's traits to the team's advantage.

Know the officials. Referees may all dress alike, but they don't all call the game alike. Is one referee whistle-happy? Is another inclined to ignore ticky-tack fouls? Does one referee follow the letter of the law when it comes to 3-seconds in the key, whereas another is led by the spirit of the rule and only makes that call if you have gained an advantage? Do the referees have any favorite calls that they like to make? Referees may be respected or hated, but they are still people. If you treat all officials with respect, you may be the one who gets the close call in your favor.

Know yourself. You need to be sensitive to your own performance. For example, are you experiencing emotional or physical problems that may cause you to be out of sync? The player with court sense doesn't try to fool himself. You know when you are not playing up to par and you want to let that knowledge influence the decisions you make during the game.

EXPECT THE UNEXPECTED

The players who know how to think the game are the ones who condition their coaches, teammates, opponents, and fans to expect the unexpected. Magic Johnson of the Los Angeles Lakers was that kind of player. In an NBA regional championship game against the Portland Trailblazers, Johnson was inbounding the ball under Portland's basket with fewer than five seconds left in the game. The Lakers were leading by one or two points. Instead of trying to get the ball to a teammate as most people would have done, Johnson carefully lofted the ball over everyone's head and the half-court line without letting it go out of bounds. By the time the Trailblazers took possession and got the ball back into their the front court, the game was over.

Court sense? You bet!

Chapter  6

LEARN TO WORK HARD

How the mind and body work together is a question to which no one has found a complete answer, but one thing is clear: the mind affects the body and the body affects the mind. In order to keep fit mentally, therefore, you need to attend to your body.
- From *Managing Your Mind: The Mental Fitness Guide*,
by Gillian Butler, Ph.D., and Tony Hope, M.D.

We've already talked about the importance of practicing hard in order to learn the fundamental skills of basketball. Now we're going to talk about a different kind of hard work—the kind of hard work it takes to keep your body in excellent physical condition.

CONDITIONING AND COURT SENSE

What does physical conditioning have to do with court sense? Simple. All the thinking skills in the world won't help you if you're too pooped to shoot the ball or run up the court. For court sense to be useful to you, you must first be able to execute—and to be able to execute, you have to be in good shape.

It's like my old Stanford runningmate and now CEO of Air Products (a $5 billion worldwide company), Harold "Hap" Wagner, says: "To be able to think while you are playing, you have to be the best conditioned athlete. If you are tired, you're not seeing enough and you're not responding accurately or timely to what is happening." Hap says this applies whether you're on the court or in the boardroom. The better conditioned you are, the more able you are to think, instead of just react.

At each level of competition, the need for conditioning is greater.

For example, if you dream of some day playing in the pros, your chances will be better if you are in top physical condition.

Even for number-one draft picks, it can be challenging to make the transition from playing college ball to playing pro ball. As Tim Duncan wrote in a column for *USA TODAY*:

> The differences between the NBA and college are becoming more and more apparent even after only eight pre-season games. At this point, it is hard to imagine playing 82 games and hopefully a lot more in the playoffs. That's about three times more than I played each year in college. Also, an NBA game is 48 minutes long. A college game is only 40. Eight minutes might not seem like much, unless you're the one playing. Plus, there is a 24-second shot clock in the NBA as opposed to a 35-second clock in college. This makes for more shots, meaning more trips up and down the court. And, of course, the NBA game is much more physical, and the players are much bigger and more skilled.

So don't make the mistake of thinking (as a lot of young players do) that once you make the team—whether it's in high school, college, or the NBA—your work is done. The truth is, it's only just begun.

IT'S NEVER TOO LATE TO START

The weightlifting strengthened my arms and really helped my serve. I should have started a program when I was younger, because it makes your body stronger and not as likely to be injured.
        - Steffi Graf, returning to tennis in 1997 after a knee injury

When training began for the 1997-98 basketball season, Karl Malone was not a happy man. After coming close to winning the title the previous season, Malone felt players should have been working extra-hard during the summer to come back in even better shape for another title run. After all, Malone himself is legendary for his summer workout regimen.

Instead, many players came back, well, a little flabby (to put things nicely). One of the players who felt Malone's wrath was Greg Ostertag, the big Utah center. Ostertag even admitted that staying in shape wasn't a top priority for him over the summer. Perhaps it should have come as no surprise when, a few games into the season, Ostertag was benched because of his poor performance.

You see, even professional athletes sometimes need to learn how important good physical conditioning is to playing well. Perhaps because they're already in such good shape, they think they don't have to put as much effort into it anymore.

Kenny Anderson knows otherwise. Kenny Anderson entered the NBA at 20, and spent four and a half lackluster seasons with the New Jersey Nets before signing a seven-year contract with the Portland Trailblazers. He said that the NBA lifestyle initially led him to make some poor decisions in his life. When he decided to turn things around, one of the things he did was to commit to getting his body in better shape. In his first year with Portland, he lost 1.5 percent of his body fat (to 5.1 percent) and gained six pounds of muscle. The increased strength helped his defense, which had been a weakness but soon went on to improve to slightly above average.

The great thing is, it's never too late to start a conditioning program. I read an article not long ago about a 70-something woman who was competing in the Huntsman Senior Games (a form of senior-citizen Olympics). Earlier in her life, the woman had had some serious health problems. Doctors did not expect her to walk again. She decided she didn't like that diagnosis, so she started working on conditioning her body. She moved from wheelchair, to walker, to cane. Today she is running marathons.

CONDITIONING GIVES YOU AN EDGE

Some of the American players might make too much out of competing on red clay. It's easy to come to the French Open and get psyched out over the surface. I have no fear of going out there and grinding it out. It's not necessarily the best player that wins, but the fitter one.
                                    - Michael Chang, champion tennis player

At one time, Chris Evert was the greatest woman tennis player in the world. Then along came Martina Navratilova. Martina was bigger and stronger, and soon outplayed Chris, becoming the world's new number-one player. Now, Chrissie could have taken her millions and retired right then and there, and no one would have thought worse of her. But that wasn't in her competitive nature. Instead, she did something that few American women were doing at the time. She hit the weight room, conditioned her body, changed her game to capitalize on her new strength, and came back to become number one again.

Conditioning, like court sense, can give you an edge against athletes whose skills are similar or equal to yours. Sometimes the edge may only be a small one, but in a world where success is often measured in fractions of seconds, that can be all the edge you need.

Michael Johnson, who broke records in the 200- and 400-meter races in the 1996 Olympics talked in his book, *Slaying the Dragon*, about why he spent 10 years improving his time by little more than a second:

> Success is found in much smaller portions than most people realize. A hundredth of a second here or sometimes a tenth there can determine the fastest man in the world. At times we live our lives on a paper-thin edge that barely separates greatness from mediocrity and success from failure.
>
> Life is often compared to a marathon, but I think it is more like being a sprinter: long stretches of hard work punctuated by brief moments in which we are given the opportunity to perform at our best.

In sports, keeping your body conditioned can protect you from serious injury and can increase your longevity as an athlete. In his mid-30s, Michael Jordan was outplaying athletes 10 years younger than himself. Would he have been able to play at that level if he didn't keep his body in shape? Probably not. Michael's conditioning has been called the bedrock of all his talents. "When I became Michael's trainer eight years ago," said trainer Tim Grover in a 1997 interview, "he was a little skeptical about working out with weights because it was something new to him. But he knew he would have to improve his conditioning program if he were to maintain his physical skills as he grew older. He said he'd seen other stars he'd idolized take to an extensive conditioning program later than they should have in their careers....So Michael started early, gradually increased his commitment and expanded a program he himself was designing with my help. And now it's a vital part of his life. It's nothing for us to arrive in a city at 2, 3 A.M. and for Jordan to be in the gym working out at 9 A.M. before the team starts its regular workouts an hour later."

"Everybody says 34 is old," Jordan said. "The challenge is to still do at 35 what the young guys are doing at 25 and 26....Consistency is the highest thing on my plate at this stage of my career. My aim is to consistently be able to go out and do my job and do it well."

WHAT DOES IT TAKE TO BE IN CONDITION?

In my years of coaching I have worked with many players and seen a variety of attitude problems. Some players are selfish. Some doubted what we were trying to do. Some weren't as committed to the team concept as they should have been. I can live with all that. What I can't live with is a player who won't work hard.
- Rick Pitino, head coach, Boston Celtics

No one gives 100%. Forget all this talk about 110%, 120%, or 200%. All players loaf. Even great ones. Push yourself, fight yourself, and make yourself hustle more and more. There's always more you can do.
- Dick DeVenzio, former Duke player,
author and basketball camp director

I see so many young players with egos out of whack. They all want to be like Mike, but they don't understand what's behind it.
- Fred Lynch, one of Michael Jordan's high school coaches

Conditioning involves physical and mental discipline. A lot of players think they have that kind of discipline, but they don't.

Jerry Rice of the San Francisco 49ers is another athlete who is famous for his commitment to conditioning. Even after all his many successes as a wide receiver, he still has a workout routine that few can keep up with. His typical daily off-season workout consists of:

- strenuous warm-up stretches
- 14 sets of stop and go's (running five yards and back, then 40 yards and back)
- six sets of triangle cones (accelerating quickly on an angle to a cone, then changing direction and heading toward another cone)
- six sets of 40-yard sprints with the ball
- 20-yard sprints until exhaustion
- weightlifting

"See, lots of guys say they want to be the best," Rice told *Sky* magazine, "but they're not willing to do the little things. I'm willing to make the sacrifices, to do the work. I mean, I dare anyone to come out and hang with me. Full out, not hold back. Seriously, there's not many out there with my endurance. Or my desire."

Dick DeVenzio used to run a basketball camp called the 87% Basketball Camp. He called it that because he hated to hear people talking about how they "gave 100%" as an athlete.

"It's all hype," DeVenzio said. "It's all garbage. No one gives everything. You can have your thousand and 500 and 200 percent. I look for the athlete who gives an honest 87 percent, who knows it and who is constantly trying to add 2 percent here and 2 percent there. I figure there's a certain complacency in the guy who calls himself a 100 percenter. I imagine he has quit thinking, quit actively searching for ways to do more, because he apparently thinks he already does everything."

Athletes with court sense recognize the importance of physical conditioning. They not only recognize its importance, but they are willing to do the hard work it takes to stay in condition.

Chapter  7

LEARN TO STAY IN CONTROL

The gem cannot be polished without friction, nor man perfected without trials.

- Chinese proverb

Staying in control is related to court sense in much the same way as staying in shape or learning the rules of the game. In each case, the player decides whether to stay in control, get in top shape, or learn the rules.

In other word, you choose whether you are going to lose your cool or keep it. No one "makes" you do it. It is always your choice.

The player who maintains self control is the one who realizes that he can hurt his team by blowing his lid. Knowing this helps him stay in control.

There are many ways an athlete can lose control. Can you think of some of them? Losing your focus is one way of losing control. Not eating right and not getting enough rest before a game are others. Depending on performance-enhancing drugs (or any kind of drugs) is still another way of giving up control.

However, the most common forms of lost self control are physical and verbal aggression.

The sports world is filled with examples of athletes who allow the wind of anger to blow out the candle of reason. To me, the most amazing examples come from professional sports. I always find these hard to understand because you'd think that professional athletes 1) would be more mature, and 2) would know better. Nevertheless, in just the short period of time while I was researching this section of the book, the following incidents occurred:

- Shaquille O'Neal knocked Greg Ostertag to the floor because

Ostertag had accused Shaq of having no class. O'Neal blamed the incident on "testosterone." I guess he had to say that because he couldn't blame it on the heat of the game, since (a) the game hadn't even started yet, and (b) O'Neal wasn't playing in the game anyway.

- Jim Harbaugh, Indianapolis Colts' quarterback, suffered a small fracture in his right hand during a fight with Jim Kelly, the ex-Buffalo Bills quarterback who is an NBC-TV analyst. Kelly criticized Harbaugh during a pregame show, calling him a "baby" who "overdramatized" injuries. So Harbaugh reportedly hit Kelly in the head during an NBC meeting at the Colts' hotel in San Diego. Harbaugh, too, went with the unconvincing "testosterone" defense. "I regret throwing the punch," Harbaugh told ESPN, "but I felt I had to do something since my toughness was being questioned."

- Charles Barkley was arrested in October 1997 for allegedly throwing a 20-year-old man through a plate-class window after the man tossed a glass of ice on him. This wasn't the first time Barkley had gotten into that kind of trouble. Two earlier incidents where Charles reportedly assaulted individuals ended with one acquittal and one case where the charges were dropped. The Barkley incidents are especially hard to understand since Charles, for all his bluster and big talk, is one of the most well liked and well respected players in the league.

- In overtime, Washington Redskins receiver Michael Westbrook threw his helmet which led to a 15-yard penalty and a missed field-goal opportunity. The Redskins went on to lose the game.

- Redskins quarterback Gus Frerotte sprained his neck when he head-butted the stadium wall to celebrate a touchdown (which shows it's not just anger that helps people lose control).

Nick Van Exel of the Los Angeles Lakers is also known for his lack of self-control. He pushed a referee. He argued publicly with his coach. But coming into the 1997-98 season, Van Exel realized that changes had to be made. "We gotta grow up now," he said. He understands that his role is to keep his emotions under control while running the team on the floor, and to allow himself to be coached—both essential ingredients of court sense.

COURT SENSE AND STAYING IN CONTROL

As Nick Van Exel noted, the ability to stay in control is a sign of maturity. The best ballplayers have this trait—the ability to stay in control in the middle of pressure and adversity. In addition to maturity, it requires intelligence, courage, and determination.

Malaika Underwood is a good example of an athlete with these qualities. As the daughter of a white father and a black mother, and as the only girl in San Diego County playing high school baseball, she has had her share of pressure. When she played for a Chollas Lake youth team, Malaika and her mostly African-American and Latino teammates endured taunts and slurs shouted at them by opposing players and their parents when they played games in mostly white areas. "Parents would yell out racial slurs from the stands. Kids would come at her very hard at second base and pitch her high and inside," said Malaika's coach.

"I just took a deep breath and realized they didn't understand what they were saying," Malaika said. "They were going on nothing but stereotypes." A very mature attitude—and one that has helped Malaika become an outstanding ballplayer and an outstanding young woman.

BUT HE CALLED ME A *#@!!

If there is one thing that makes the sports world different from anything else, it's the fact that not only are you involved in intense physical competition, but you also have a lot of people watching you while you're doing it. Sure, politicians and celebrities have people watching them all the time, but not while they're playing in the heat of a physical contest that could determine their very livelihood. Of course, I'm not saying these things are excuses for losing control. What I'm saying is that you have to recognize that if you are involved in sports, these are situations that are going to challenge your sense of control. You need to be prepared to deal with them.

Fans. Golfer Greg Norman, a pro for over 20 years, has acknowledged that it can be difficult to keep your cool in the middle of competition. Fans can be especially troublesome when you're trying to stay focused. The spectators make comments, the players hear them, then try to not react to what is being said. "I think all sports have changed," said Norman. "The media coverage is more intense, so the people feel like they know you. They feel like they can come up and say whatever they want to say to you."

Trash talk. In years past, trash talk consisted of a casual comment here and there. But things have changed. Now the trend is to humiliate your opponent. Karl Malone said, "I've had guys say something about every part of my life except my wife and family." One of the hardest things to do is to ignore the taunting and trash talk that goes on in a sporting event. You don't have to ignore it, however—just use it to inspire yourself to a better performance. As Malone said, "I get it back on the floor."

Officials. All-Star second baseman Roberto Alomar claimed he lost control and spit at umpire John Hirschbeck because, after ejecting Alomar from a key game, the umpire then said some nasty things to Alomar. "He said something strong, but I should never have done what I did," Alomar admitted. "I'm not going to sit here and say what I did was right. It wasn't right. But it was emotional and in the heat of the moment." If you have trouble accepting authority, or are convinced the referee is out to get you or your team, it can be hard to stay in control when a call is made against you. But if you lose control, you are punishing your team as well as yourself.

THE HIGH COST OF "LOSING IT"

We don't condone those actions. He put the whole team in jeopardy. Our position is "team first."

> - Baltimore Colts vice president Bill Tobin,
> speaking about the Jim Harbaugh incident

Tony's always under control, and he wants his players to be that way, too.

- Herman Edwards, assistant head coach of the
Tampa Bay Buccaneers, talking about
head coach Tony Dungy

If you play for the Tampa Bay Buccaneers, one of the team rules you soon learn about is "no fighting." Forget that rule and you can forget about practice—it's off to the locker room for you. Maintaining your composure, even during practices, is something that coach Tony Dungy often talks to his players about. Dungy believes that if you lose your cool on the practice field, you'll lose your cool in games. And that can be costly.

What are some of the consequences of "losing it?" Team and individual fines. Suspensions. Serious, even career-threatening injuries. Loss of respect. Resentment from your teammates. Ejection from the game. Penalties and fouls that can lose a game or a championship.

You need to remember that when you're playing on a team, you're not out there playing for yourself. If you lose control, it doesn't just affect you—it affects your team, too.

After receiving a one-game suspension for his actions against Greg Ostertag, Shaquille O'Neal admitted that he had been wrong. "I made a mistake," he said. "Instead of focusing upon what is best for the team, I got caught up in the drama of the season's first game and reacted emotionally instead of logically. I acknowledge my responsibility to set a good example for young people and I admit that in this instance, I did not do so. I ask those young people not to emulate my conduct here because there is no excuse to engage in physical confrontation."

CONTROL PAYS OFF

The last year or so, he's learned to control his emotions. That's a major part of pitching. Now he's a left-hander with good stuff and a good head.

- San Francisco Giants pitching coach Dick Pole,
speaking of pitcher Shawn Estes

Before I had to get it—and get it right now. Every game had to be a no-hit shut-out....As I look back, I wouldn't have wanted to be on a team with me. I was never on a winning team when I was the guy. I never came through. I wasn't a winner. You could say I choked—I always gave in to the pressure.

— Shawn Estes, pitcher

Not only does staying in control pay off in terms of fewer penalties and injuries, it also helps you play better. For example, early in his career, pitcher Shawn Estes played with such emotion and intensity that it wasn't good for him. The littlest mistake would get him upset and throw his game off. Until he started learning how to control and channel his feelings, Estes was stuck in the minor leagues.

Being able to stay in control is a sign of mental toughness. Just look at the great players—such as Michael Jordan and Magic Johnson. Or take Tim Duncan, who in his first year as a professional basketball player exhibited more maturity and control than many long-standing veterans. These are individuals who know the value of being mentally tough.

THE MENTALLY TOUGH ATHLETE

If you want to be a top competitor, you have to be more than physically tough. You have to be mentally tough. At the core of mental toughness is the ability to control your emotional responses and concentrate on what needs to be done. The mentally tough athlete is relaxed under fire. They are at their best when the pressure is on.

Mental toughness is not something you're born with. It is a set of specific, learned attitudes and skills. You learn to be mentally tough by surviving the hard or unfair things that happen to you in life. For example, the first time you fall in love and get your heart broken, you think you're never going to be able to survive. But you do. The next time you suffer a broken heart, it's no less painful—but you know that you survived it once and you can survive it again.

Mental toughness is something you carry with you always—not just when you're playing. It's a quality of mind that allows you to do your best without complaining about the little things. Mentally tough players look at themselves and at pressure situations in ways that bring out their best. Mentally tough players know how to successfully handle the stress that comes with playing sports.

THE STRESS TEST

What is stress? A synonym for stress is "change." That change can be positive (such as making the varsity squad) or negative (being cut from the team). Either way, it is something that throws you out of your comfort zone and forces you to adapt to something new.

Every athlete is tested by stress. But not every athlete reacts the same way to stress. The ability to handle pressure, or stress, is a mark of mental toughness.

Why do some people explode and some don't? There are lots of reasons. The physical and mental tests that some see as opportunities or challenges, others see as threats. Some athletes see pressure situations as a challenge to rise to the occasion. Other athletes feel that their athletic performance is a reflection of their own self-worth. Therefore, they have a great need to avoid failing. They are so threatened by the fear of failure that they choke, or react inappropriately.

Athletes with low self-esteem are also more likely to lose control when they are faced with stress. When you have low self-esteem, it usually means you don't value yourself enough to control your impulses for your own sake.

Stress affects all athletes, from the peewees to the pros. Positive, or good, stress is helpful in preparing you for competition. It gets your juices going. Bad stress happens when the level of intensity causes distress and affects your performance negatively. When stress levels exceed your personal limits, these consequences can occur:

- staleness, or loss of enthusiasm
- overtraining
- physical and mental exhaustion
- lack of sleep
- depression
- anger
- burnout

Learn to Stay in Control

There are lots of books and tapes available that teach you how to handle stress in a positive way, so we won't go into the subject in-depth in this book. However, there are a few points I would like to make about handling stress that comes from athletic competition:

(1) When playing sports, there is one sentence that you should always remember: It's only a game. There are a lot worse things that could happen to you than losing a basketball contest.

(2) To help yourself handle stress better, emphasize effort and improvement, not winning. Often, whether you win or lose is beyond your control. What you can control is how you perform. Focus on your skills, not on what the score is or what happened on the previous play.

(3) A lot of times you hear coaches say, "So-and-so needs to play more aggressively." What they really mean is that person needs to play more assertively. There is a difference between aggression and assertion. Aggression is emotional, out of control. It's hard to channel. Assertiveness is about setting goals, knowing tasks and methods to reach them, and using your brain. Be an assertive player, not an aggressive one.

(4) Recognize where your hot buttons are. For Charles Barkley, it's when he feels like he isn't being respected. Nick Van Exel has problems with authority—whether it's his coach or an official. Everyone has different hot buttons. Find yours. Then make a plan. Figure out exactly what you will do if your buttons get pushed. I don't mean thinking, "I'm gonna smash that (bleep) in the face if he says that to me again." I mean you need to think of a constructive way to use your emotions.

(5) Accept responsibility. Recognize that you can control your actions. Too many people today blame others for their own bad behavior. When Vancouver forward Shareef Abdur-Rahim was asked if he thought he would have any problems dealing with the NBA's new female referees, Shareef said: "No. It kind of really keeps you good because you don't want to say anything. I've got a mother and sisters,

so I don't want to say anything to one of them (the female officials) that I wouldn't say to my sisters or my mother." Shareef makes a point that too few athletes realize: When you have the right motivation, you can control yourself.

SELF-CONTROL: THE HIDDEN WEAPON

So far, we have talked about how an athlete with court sense can use his or her own self-control to play a better game. Now let's talk about another example of court sense in action: that's the athlete who takes advantage of an opponent's "short fuse" or lack of self-assurance.

Often a player will deliberately upset a key player on the other team, either to throw off his game or get him thrown out of the game. I will never forget the story my high school coach, Ken Fagans, told us about such an incident. He was an outstanding player at Oregon State and they were playing in a championship game. A third-stringer started for the opposing team and promptly slugged Fagans, who retaliated. Both players were thrown out of the game—depriving the other team of a third stringer and Oregon State of their best player.

Another example was the "stage whisper" by Chicago Bulls star, Scottie Pippen, to Utah Jazz mainstay, Karl Malone, as Malone was at the free-throw line in the closing seconds of the first game of the 1997 NBA championship. Pippen's commented something to the effect that the "Mailman (Malone's nickname) didn't deliver on Sunday." The strategy worked. Malone missed both free throws, and Utah lost the game. All the time, Malone had a history of poor free-throw shooting, and Pippen took timely advantage of his opponent's self-doubts.

You also use court sense when you somehow feel that a teammate is close to losing control, and you step in to reassure or calm the person down. You see a catcher do this when they call time-out to talk to their pitcher.

The use of court sense to either unnerve an opponent or settle down a teammate requires an artful sense of timing and tactics. Scottie Pippen didn't resort to trash talk when he baited Karl Malone, because Malone's the sort of player who uses that kind of stuff to get fired up. Likewise, the catcher with field sense doesn't run out to the mound at the first bad throw his pitcher makes. That would signal a lack of confidence in the pitcher.

There is no formula for knowing what to say or do or when to do it. Like many aspects of court sense, this knowledge comes with experience and awareness. By staying alert and watching for opportunities, you, too, can learn to use this tool to your advantage.

YOU CAN STAY IN CONTROL AND STILL HAVE FUN

Finally, let me emphasize that being in control doesn't mean being emotionless. It means using your emotions in a positive way. For example, I wish someone had told me that it was okay to be nervous before the game. For some reason, I saw nervousness as something bad, and the fact that I was nervous meant I wasn't as in control as I thought I should be. I wasted too much energy worrying about my nervousness. Now, if I had wanted to, I could have turned that nervousness around. I could have seen those butterflies in the stomach as a sign that my body was getting ready for something exciting—another challenge, another opportunity.

Sports should be enjoyable, and you should be able to enjoy the feelings that come through playing sports. Because as you get older—especially once your playing days are over—you will experience those twinges of excitement and anticipation less and less often. So enjoy it now while you can!

Chapter  8

LEARN TO DEVELOP CHARACTER

We're not looking for players who are characters; we're looking for players who have character.

- Motto on a locker room wall

The best people make the best players.

- Sportswriter Jack McCallum, talking
about Joe Dumars of the Detroit Pistons

WHAT IS CHARACTER?

When I was growing up, one of my favorite radio programs was "The Lone Ranger," which was later made into a successful TV series. The main characters (if you're not familiar with them) were a masked white man, called the Long Ranger, and his American Indian companion,Tonto. Together they battled cattle rustlers, horse thieves, bank robbers and other assorted bad guys.

Why did I like the Lone Ranger so much? One reason is because you could always depend on him to do the right thing. It wasn't like a lot of shows today, where the good guys aren't always good and the bad guys aren't always bad. You knew exactly where you stood with the Lone Ranger. He had character.

The creator of "The Lone Ranger" was Francis H. Striker. In a recent book entitled *The Lone Ranger's Code of the West*, Striker's son talked about what his father wanted to accomplish in writing the Lone Ranger stories. There were certain values that Striker wanted young people to understand and adopt for themselves. These included courage, respect, loyalty, honesty, fairness, compassion, tolerance, and duty. Each of the radio and television episodes focused on one or more of these qualities.

Learn to Develop Character

According to the ancient Greeks, the qualities of character included courage, temperance (or self-control), justice, and wisdom. Early Catholic scholars added prudence, or carefulness, to the list.

Today, most would agree that trustworthiness, respect, responsibility, honesty, fairness, and caring for others are essential parts of good character.

But does character really matter when you're playing sports? After all, there are plenty of examples of successful athletes with big character flaws. For the most part, however, these are athletes whose physical skills are so excellent that they outweigh just about everything else.

For athletes who don't have those kinds of physical skills, and certainly for any athlete who plays team sports, I think character matters a lot. There are even certain sports, like the martial arts, where character is as important as physical skill. For example, tae kwon do teaches the importance of integrity, perseverance, courtesy, self-control, and indomitable spirit, along with self-defense techniques.

Why is character important? Your character determines how you respond to temptations and challenges in life. It determines how you act when things get tough. Unlike reputation, which is what people think you are, character is what you really are.

A lot of athletes who make it to the pros may be good, but they will never reach the level of a Michael Jordan. It's not because they don't have the athleticism or the knowledge of the fundamentals of their sport. It's because they don't have the character. They don't have the same desire to work hard, and same sense of respect for and responsibility to the game and for their teammates.

When you lack character, you will never be able to become a complete player—at least, not by my definition. That's because to be a complete player, you must have good character to go along with your court sense, athleticism, and mastery of the basic skills of your sport.

WHAT DOES CHARACTER HAVE TO DO WITH COURT SENSE?

Remember, success in life is not reserved for the most talented, for people with the highest IQs or people with the most ability. Success is almost totally dependent on character, courage, desire, drive and persistence.

- from A Strategy for Winning, by Carl Mays

Although I realize that I'm not going to win in the NFL without some extraordinary skilled players, character has always been just as important to me—and in some cases, more important.

- Don Shula, former NFL coach

If court sense means learning to think in the most effective and efficient way possible in the game, then how does character help you do that? Here's one way: When you've already decided that you are someone who plays by the rules, you don't have to take time to ask yourself, "Should I do this? Should I do that? Should I undercut my opponent? Should I go for the hard foul?" Those questions have already been answered, and those decisions made. That saves a lot of time, and allows you to be a more effective player.

As we talked about in the previous section, self-control is an important element of court sense. When you have a strong character, you are also better able to control your emotions for the sake of others. You realize that when you behave badly on the court, you will be penalized, and that penalty can affect your whole team.

Over the years, we have learned that when a person has a set of values and sticks to them, more often than not that person has more productivity, harmony, fulfillment, and profitability in all areas of life—not just sports.

People who live by the values mentioned above—respect, responsibility, and so on—generally have more self-discipline than people who don't have those values.

Coaches know that character and court sense often go together. As Carl Mays wrote in his book, *A Strategy for Winning*: "When a coach comes down to a crucial part of the game, he doesn't choose just anybody. He chooses someone he knows has character. Someone he knows has courage. Someone he knows has a strong possibility of coming through when it's needed. And what's true in sports is true in all other areas of life."

Learn to Develop Character

HOW DO YOU DEVELOP CHARACTER?

I wasn't excessively competitive—I don't think my folks would've allowed it. They stressed other things besides winning. Life always was about more than that. I had to be a good person. When I lost, I had to shake the other guy's hand.
- Barry Sanders, Detroit Lions running back
and Heisman Trophy winner

Sports do not build character—they reveal it.
- Heywood Hale Broun

When it comes to developing character, some athletes—like Barry Sanders—are lucky enough to have families who teach the values that matter. However, there are plenty of kids from good homes who grow up to have flawed characters, and there are plenty of kids from not-so-good homes who grow up to have strong characters.

There are many things a player can do that will help strengthen and develop character. These include: defining your values; taking responsibility for your actions; choosing your friends carefully; and learning to be a leader.

DEFINE YOUR VALUES

I think for a long time in professional sports we represented—owners, franchises and players—something to our society to aspire to. We represented things about accepting challenges, playing through adversity. In short, we were role models. I fear we have become just a reflection of our society and don't create the higher vision, the higher value, the higher dream.
- Larry Miller, owner, Utah Jazz

Successful people have clear values. When we make mistakes in life, it's often because we have strayed from those values. Have you taken the time to examine your life and the values that drive your daily behavior? If you were invited to give a speech about your values, what would you say?

Values help you to make sense of the world. Every decision you make is based on your values. Values can be compared to basketball fundamentals. Values are life fundamentals. They are the things you always fall back on. They are the things that make you a better player.

Sports can help you decide what values are important to you. NBA Star Anfernee "Penny" Hardaway said, "Sports played a major role in keeping me on the right track by teaching me discipline, respect for myself and others."

What kind of values have you learned from sports? Are they good values (hard work, fair play) or harmful values (win at any cost)? It is easy to get away from the basics in the game and in life—in this case, the basics being your personal values. Take the time to think about what your values are, or what you would like them to be.

TAKE RESPONSIBILITY FOR YOUR ACTIONS

My experience has always been that the quality people that win you the championships are the same people that want the discipline, that want the organization, and that are the first to modify their behavior to the rules.

- Bill Walton, former NBA star

They hurt a lot of other people when this happens, it's not just them. It affects a lot of other people. You must have empathy for them. But they must also understand that when they do wrong, they must pay the price.

- John Wooden, former UCLA basketball coach,
speaking of UCLA's indefinite suspension of starters
Kris Johnson and Jelani McCoy for unspecified violations

Everyone has heard the story about George Washington and the cherry tree. Did the young Washington really chop down a tree and then tell the truth about doing it? Who knows? The story is important, though, because it points out a valuable aspect of George Washington's character. He was seen as someone who, if he did something wrong, had the strength of character to admit his mistake. He took responsibility for his actions.

Learn to Develop Character

In the section on "Learn to Think the Game," I talked about knowing how and when to use the rules creatively, even break the rules. However, I should make something clear. When I talked about breaking the rules, I meant breaking the rules in order to take advantage of the penalty that comes with it. I didn't mean you should break the rules with the hope of avoiding a penalty. When you break the rules in order to try to get away with something, you are not being responsible.

Unfortunately, athletes—in any sport—break rules the way most people break the speed limit at one time or another. Athletes often have the attitude, "It's only wrong if I'm caught."

"If you're a decent basketball player, you're pushed into it," said Terrance Roberson, a three-time Parade All-American who sat out his freshman year at Fresno State in 1995-96 after his ACT test score was challenged. "You're thinking, if I don't pass this test, I might not be in school. I might still be around the neighborhood. You're going to do whatever it takes. In this world, if you ain't got caught, you ain't cheating."

Sometimes cheating is even coached. I read about one NFL coach who would tell his players, "If you ain't cheatin, you ain't tryin."

However, I believe that a little cheating (sneaking a look at test answers, lying to your coach) leads to bigger cheating. Anytime you cheat, you lose a little bit of your self-esteem, because you know you haven't accomplished things by your own efforts.

Golfer Barclay Howard was playing in the U.S. Amateur Championships in 1997 when he discovered he had broken the rule that said you could only play with one kind of ball. No one else knew he had broken the rule. He certainly hadn't done it on purpose—it was just an accidental thing. Howard could have kept quiet and no one would have known. Instead, he reported the violation and had himself disqualified. "I would know," Howard said. "Say I was walking up to win on this weekend, how could I live with myself? After 44 years, you're going to start cheating? No. It's disappointing because I made the cut. Here I am looking forward to match play and all of a sudden I'm out. At my age, you don't know how many chances you'll get. But you learn from your mistakes, don't you? You see, even at 44 years of age, I'm still learning."

Howard took responsibility for his actions, even though they were unintentional. He knew that winning by cheating—even if he was the only one who ever found out—would make him feel wrong. He knew it would diminish his character.

Not every athlete feels the same way, though. In a 1995 poll of athletes, most of them U.S. Olympians or aspiring Olympians, the question was asked: "You are offered a banned performance-enhancing substance, with two guarantees: 1) You will not be caught; 2) You will win. Would you take the substance?" One-hundred-ninety-five athletes said yes; only three said no.

Sometimes taking responsibility for your actions means standing up to those who would have you do otherwise. In the operating room of a large, well-known hospital, a young nurse was completing her first day of full responsibility. "You've only removed eleven sponges, doctor," she said to the surgeon. "We used twelve."

"I removed them all," the doctor said. "We'll close the incision now."

"No," the nurse objected. "We used twelve sponges."

"I'll take the responsibility," the surgeon said grimly. "Suture!"

"You can't do that!" the nurse insisted. "Think of the patient."

The surgeon smiled, lifted his foot, and showed the nurse the twelfth sponge. "You'll do," he said.

CHOOSE YOUR FRIENDS CAREFULLY

Winners must surround themselves with positive, uplifting people who share the same values. One of the most important things a person can do is choose associates wisely. We seem to take on the characteristics of those around us and become much like them. So the friends we choose are important in helping us develop positive values.

- from A Strategy for Winning, by Carl Mays

You get the feeling he thinks he'd be selling out if he distanced himself from some of the people he came up with. I used to tell him he didn't have to turn his back on where he came from, but he had to be strong enough to say, "Look, fellas, I can't go with you to this place, or I can't

do that with you. Because if something happens, if the cops come, it's going to be me getting in the paper." He'd always nod his head and tell me I was right, but did I get through? I'd have to say no."
- Kevin McHale, talking about Isaiah Rider
of the Portland Trailblazers

I do have a little posse, though. It consists of my friend Mario Joyner, who is a financial advisor for Merrill Lynch here in Detroit, and my childhood friend Mike Ellison, who works with Sports Marketing Network. Not to knock anyone else who might have a posse, but these guys are professionals and motivated to succeed and don't want to be known as Grant Hill's boys. They want to be known as individuals. That's my posse.
- Grant Hill, Detroit Pistons

Like it or not, your character is reflected in the people you hang with. I think that's part of Allen Iverson's image problem. He was raised in the projects and still hangs out with his friends from those times. That loyalty is commendable. However, you have to realize that if your friends do something wrong and you're with them, it will reflect on you. (In other words, you may not be smoking, but you'll still smell like smoke.) There's a fine line to be drawn. I think the answer lies in having the strength to let your friends know what your values are. If they want to be around you, they have to show respect for your values. If they're really your friends, they will.

Sometimes, though, you may have to give up certain relationships in order to maintain your values. Bobby Jackson, a star player for the University of Minnesota's Final Four team in 1997, grew up in a drug-infested, violence-ridden housing project in Salisbury, North Carolina. After playing for Western Nebraska Community College, Jackson chose to play for Minnesota. He could have easily played closer to home, but he didn't care to fall back under the spell of some questionable acquaintances. No wonder Minnesota coach Clem Haskins had this to say about Jackson: "I recruited him because of his ability, but he's even a better person than a basketball player."

LEARN TO BE A LEADER

Whether they want to be or don't want to be, players are role models and enlightened people recognize that.

- NFL President Neil Austrian

People with character will always be leaders. Sometimes they are outspoken leaders. Other times they are quiet leaders, who don't even think of themselves as leaders, but who lead by example. No matter what their personality, good leaders share certain qualities. These include: the willingness to work as a team, the courage to stand up for what they believe, and the desire to help others.

LEADERS ARE TEAM PLAYERS

Each player must be eager, not just willing, to sacrifice personal glory for the welfare of the team.

- John Wooden

I came down ... hard on Shaquille O'Neal .... because I thought it was important he be publicly embarrassed. From now on, I want Shaq to think twice. He is a team leader. He is a great athlete. But if everybody lets him get away with everything, he will never be all that he can be.

- Mike Downey, sportswriter for the Los Angeles Times

Everything on our team is run for Keith, through Keith or is about Keith, but you wouldn't know it. Keith is the first guy to practice, the first guy to every team meeting. He's the best captain I've ever had because he leads by example and he also has such great concern for his teammates. Keith is just very special.

- Rick Majerus, University of Utah coach, talking about his top NBA draft pick, Keith Van Horn

Leaders put the team first. They work to make their teammates better, not just themselves.

Learn to Develop Character

Shawn Kemp is an outstanding athlete in terms of physical athleticism, but when it came to being a team player for the Seattle SuperSonics, he fell short. His habit of being late all the time threw the team off. A month before the 1997 playoffs, during one seven-day period, Kemp was late for almost every team function. He missed the team flight to Phoenix and missed practice that same afternoon. He was late for a team meeting a few days later and then missed another practice. What kind of message do you think that sent to the other players? It says, I don't care enough about you to be on time. Small wonder that Kemp was eventually traded.

Isaiah (J.R.) Rider is another player with a lateness problem. As one writer noted: "He set the tone for his career by arriving hours late for his first practice as a pro....Since then he has missed or been late for more practices, bus rides and flights than his coaches care to count." Rider is also a player who has caused turmoil on his team, despite his natural physical talents. His career in the NBA has been marked by fines, suspensions, and even arrests.

Rider's behavior was so disruptive that the Minnesota Timberwolves traded him—cheap—to the Portland Trailblazers. "I like J.R., I really do," said Timberwolves vice president of basketball operations Kevin McHale. "Ninety-five percent of the time he's a great guy to be around. But it got to the point where every couple of weeks it was another incident, and we just couldn't depend on him. It's like having a friend who's always late to pick you up. You still want him as a friend, but after a while you stop asking him for a ride."

Why is teamwork so important? Let me just offer a couple of examples. First, do you know why birds fly in a "V" formation? Birds fly in a "V" because when they do, they can fly 71 percent farther than birds who don't. That's because the lead bird cuts through the wind, creating a back draft for the other birds. That way, the flock gets less tired and is able to fly farther.

Second example: There was a weight-pulling contest among horses in a small, southern Canadian town. The first-place winner pulled 8,000 pounds. The second place horse pulled 7,000 pounds. The contest organizer decided to see what the two horses could pull together. The spectators were amazed as the two horses pulled 32,000 pounds.

Leaders are team players because they know they can accomplish more that way.

When it comes to playing team sports, I believe there are four levels of players:

Level One: Non-participant, non-player
Players at this level are physically present but mentally absent.

Level Two: Participant player
Players at this level are both physically and mentally in the game.

Level Three: Self-coached player
The self-coached player is a self-leader and self-learner. Basically, he's motivated to play for himself.

Level Four: Team player, team builder
This is the highest level a player can be. You do your best for the team.

Players with court sense strive to be Level Four players. One way you can do this is to encourage your teammates in their play. I know I always shot better when I felt the encouragement of my teammates. Encouragement does make a difference. You will probably never re-alize how big of an impact you can have on another person just by encouraging them.

How can you encourage your teammates? One of the most impor-tant ways is to be an example of someone who puts the team first. Behavioral experts say 95% of what we learn comes from watching others. As your teammates watch you and see you passing the ball instead of shooting it, or taking the time to help someone with their shot, then they will know that you are a team player.

Grant Hill knows what it's like to be an example. He also knows what it's like to learn from an example. When a reporter asked him what it was like hanging out with some of the members of the Olym-pic Dream Team, Hill mentioned one player who was a good example for him.

Karl Malone is about winning and doing it the right way. I try to emulate him and do whatever it takes to make my team better and help win games. Maybe that's why I have so many triple-doubles. I don't go out and try to get them. I just go out and play. I had a lot of games where I was one assist or one rebound away....The offense goes through me, so I have the opportunity to get triple-doubles. But believe me, you can't think about getting them because I've had them and we've lost. A triple-double doesn't mean a whole lot when you lose.

Other things you can do to encourage your teammates include helping them reach their goals, setting specific team goals, giving teammates immediate and specific feedback, and developing team values that are honest, positive, and optimistic. By doing these things, you do more than just help your teammates. You show yourself to be a player with character.

LEADERS HAVE COURAGE

I'd rather be compared with him as a person than as an athlete.
                              - Jesse Simms, star football player and
                        grandson of baseball great Jackie Robinson

When Branch Ricky, owner of the Brooklyn Dodgers, met with Jackie Robinson (the man who became the first black player in major league baseball), he said, "I need more than a great player. I need a man who will accept insults, take abuse, in a word, carry the flag for his race. Can you do it? I know you are naturally combative, but for three years—three years—you will have to do it the only way it can be done. Three years? Can you do it?"

Robinson said, "Mr. Rickey, do you want a player who's afraid to fight back?"

Rickey said, "I want a player with guts enough not to fight back."

As on writer described it, Robinson was "a man with sufficient strength of character to overcome abuse without surrendering his dignity and the physical ability to play baseball at a level high enough to prove he belonged."

Robinson had to deal with abuse from fans, other players, his own teammates, team owners, and the media. But he hung tough. Don Newcombe, another black player who entered the league after Jackie, said that the black players even believed that people were trying to set them up with women and get them in compromising positions—anything to get blacks out of the league. "Thank God for Jackie," Newcombe said. "He made it work."

Leaders have courage. They have the courage to do what they know is right. They have the courage to exercise self-control in the face of overwhelming temptation. And they have the courage to always keep playing at their highest level, no matter what else is going on in their lives.

Jesse Simms, Jackie Robinson's grandson, has said that his grandmother and mother always taught him that his grandfather's biggest triumph was not in sports but in leadership. It was Robinson's intelligence and character, not just his athletic skill, that helped him to become the legend that he is. As Branch Rickey recognized, there were plenty of black players with the physical talent to play baseball in the major leagues. But he needed more than that. He needed someone who could lead the others—and that quality was harder to find.

LEADERS TAKE CARE OF OTHERS

I believe you can make a real social contribution playing football.
- Steve Young

Leaders take care of other people. Sometimes that means taking the time to talk to a classmate who's not very popular. Sometimes it means donating millions of dollars to a worthy cause.

David Robinson is an example of someone who knows how to be a leader in small ways and big ways. "I generally think people are special, you know. God created everybody in His image. If it's at all possible, I need to give them the courtesy of being decent," said Robinson, explaining his patience with all the people who ask him for autographs. But Robinson does more than just sign autographs. Recently, he and his wife donated $5 million through the David Robinson Foundation to build a school in a poor area of San Antonio's almost entirely black and

Hispanic East Side. Like Robinson himself, the school will focus on character, moral development, and personal responsibility.

For whatever reason, athletes are looked up to by a lot of people. You have a choice—you can use that fame to do good, to do bad, or to do nothing. Leaders choose to do good.

FIVE GOOD WAYS TO GO BAD

Now, of course, you can always decide that this business of developing character is too much work and you'd really rather not bother. In which case, I'd like to offer you "Five Good Ways to Go Bad." Follow these tips, and you're guaranteed to avoid developing the kind of character that would make you a leader on and off the court.

(1) **Focus solely on sports**.

Super sports agent Leigh Steinberg encourages his top athletes (including Steve Young and Troy Aikman) to get involved in good causes. As Steinberg said, "The enemy for athletes is self-absorption."

(2) **Let others take care of you**.

Too many times athletes are let off the hook for their bad behavior. If you don't care about developing your character, then go ahead and take advantage of being an athlete. Let someone else do your homework. Let your brothers and sisters do your chores while you shoot baskets. Never lift a finger if you can get someone else to lift it for you.

(3) **Play for money and the awards**.

Not long ago, ESPN gathered several professional athletes and sports officials to discuss the issue of "Sportsmanship in the '90s." Few of those who appeared on the show believe that the increasing trend toward bad behavior in sports will end anytime soon. They blamed it on the need to make a living and rush of adrenaline. Some pointed the finger at television's obsession with action highlights. A few even hinted that money and the drive to win plays a role.

(4) **Buy into the media hype**.

Not long ago, I saw an advertisement for some inspirational posters that were supposed to pay tribute to "the mental power that an athlete must master." Poster number one had a close-up of a mean-looking football player, with the caption: "You're either part of the steamroller or a part of the pavement."

Poster number two showed a female volleyball player. The caption read: "You run like a girl. You hit like a girl. You throw like a girl. You serve 60 MPH in their face like a girl."

What message do these ads send? Certainly not one of sportsmanship, that's for sure.

(5) **Win at all costs**.

A children's dentist and his son were sentenced to community service and probation because dear old dad helped his son sharpen the buckle on his football helmet before a big game. Five football players were cut in the incident.

CHARACTER ENDURES

Fame is a vapor, popularity an accident, riches take wings, those who cheer today may curse tomorrow, only one thing endures—character.
- Horace Greeley

From charges that athletes gambled on sporting events, to arrests for drunken driving, rape, robbery, and assault, sports in America are seen as having a real need for some kind of moral direction. This is a tragic situation, because I believe that every athlete has dreams of being the best—or at least, the best that they can be. And I don't believe you can do that unless you have the character to guide you.

When Hall-of-Fame Dodger catcher Roy Campanella died of a heart attack at age 71, after spending the last 35 years of his life in a wheelchair, one sportswriter commented: "He had been a great ballplayer, one of the best ever at his position. But in the final analysis, he was an even better human being."

In the final analysis, you need to remember that you will not be an athlete forever. When your back is shot and your knees don't bend well anymore, and you could no more do a reverse layup than a triple back flip off the high dive, what will you have left? Your character.

PART THREE

HOW DO YOU
COACH COURT SENSE?

Chapter 9

IMPROVING YOUR EFFECTIVENESS AS A COACH

We begin with the hypothesis that any subject can be taught effectively in some intellectually honest form to any child at any stage of development.

- Jerome Bruner

Until now, I've primarily directed this book toward athletes who want to improve their playing skills by learning court sense. This section, however, is for coaches who would like to know how to coach something as intangible as court sense.

Most coaches I know of—at least, those that coach at the high school and middle school levels—are overworked and underpaid. When they get to practice, their biggest concern is what to teach that particular day, whether it be fundamentals, drills, or whatever. There is little time left to worry about HOW to teach those things. For the most part, coaches teach the same way they learned.

However, to be a more effective coach and teacher, you need to spend some time examining how you teach. Why?

(1) Old teaching methods simply do not work as well as they used to. New research has greatly expanded our knowledge of how people learn. And yet, for the most part our school systems are years behind in adapting this knowledge to the classroom.

(2) Today's student-athlete has different expectations and needs. In an article in the *Los Angeles Times* about the record number of NBA teams heading for losing seasons in 1997-98, Utah Jazz coach Jerry Sloan attributed some of the problems to the youth and inexperience of many of the players. "Some of the teams that are losing, you look at the number of first-round picks on the team." Sloan noted that today's

players tend to be "more fragile with personal things than they've been" in the past, which might explain why some of them have a hard time handling the pressure of being drafted onto a bad team. Also, because more talented players are leaving school early to become pros, ever younger players are finding their way into the NBA.

As Jerry Sloan pointed out, kids are different than they were a generation ago. They face different challenges. They view sports in a different way. Many of them have grown up without a strong authority figure in the home, which can make it difficult for them to accept authority from their coach.

To put it simply, teaching and coaching methods that may have worked well 10 or 20 years ago aren't as effective today. One example of this is the controversy that erupted between Latrell Sprewell of the Golden State Warriors, and his coach, P.J. Carlesimo.

To briefly recap the events: The Warriors had been having a lousy season, made worse by the ongoing feud between their coach and their star player (Sprewell). One day in practice, Carlesimo commented to Sprewell that his passes needed to be crisper. Sprewell got upset, physically attacked the coach, and threatened to kill him. The Warriors promptly terminated Sprewell's $32 million contract, and the NBA suspended him for a year without pay.

Of course, the Sprewell/Carlesimo incident didn't just suddenly happen out of nowhere. Sprewell had a reputation for being volatile, and Carlesimo had a reputation as a screamer who was constantly in his players' faces. Screaming, of course, is nothing new to coaches. Many of them feel that it's as much a part of the game as the basketball itself. Many very successful coaches have been noted screamers.

More and more, though, coaches are encountering players for whom yelling and screaming is not a motivational tool. As Bay Area sportscaster Gary Radnich observed, "Carlesimo comes from the old school where you do your yelling and after practice you're friends again. But name me a millionaire in any walk of life who wants to have someone yell at him."

Here's another example of how the player/coach relationship has changed over the years: Indiana coach Bobby Knight has been in the news several times lately not only for his displays of temper, but also because key players keep leaving his program to go play someplace less stressful. Many people also believe that Knight's half-court offense—once thought to be brilliant—is now too slow for a game that has speeded up and become more improvisational and creative.

Before you can teach a player court sense, you need to examine your coaching skills. Do they need updating? Are there some things you can change or do better in order to reach all of your players—not just some or most of them?

As someone who has spent a lot of time as a player and a coach, there are four areas of coaching that I think coaches need to pay special attention to before they even get to the stuff about how to sink a basket. These areas are: coaching for communication; coaching for learning; coaching for transfer; and coaching by example.

COACHING FOR COMMUNICATION

I had a friend many years ago ... I'd rather talk to him than anyone else about the game. He knew more about basketball, his knowledge was superior, better than anyone I ever knew. But he was not a successful coach because he was not a good teacher. There's a big difference between knowing the game and being able to communicate that information.

- John Wooden

Years ago you could tell a player to run through a wall and he'd do it. Now he's going to ask you, "Why do I have to run through that wall?" And if you can give him the answer, then he'll do it.

- Bobby Ross, head coach, Detroit Lions

The nature of the business is that it's a yelling business. You have to get the players' attention.

- Don Nelson, Dallas Mavericks coach and general manager

More coaches lose their jobs because of communication problems than because of their win/loss record. As John Wooden noted, all the basketball knowledge in the world won't do you any good if you can't communicate that knowledge to your players in a way that they can understand.

Communication is more than just talking, of course. As a rule, teachers outtalk their students by a ration of 3:1. I would guess for coaches the ratio would be even higher. Successful communication involves several things:

C —— Caring

Caring means knowing and supporting your athletes. This means having the self-discipline and self-control to work at a pace where athletes can learn. It means doing the little things that let your players know where they stand. For example, Phoenix Suns coach Danny Ainge lets his players' families travel on road trips. Seattle's George Karl thought about hiring a female assistant coach, because of the large number of players who were raised by single mothers. "We've got to do more for players than just pay them to play basketball," Karl said. That attitude communicates a lot to a player. It also explains why some coaches can get away with being confrontational—they back it up with a real feeling of caring and wanting their players to be better for their own sakes.

O —— Openness

To help the athlete learn and grow, you must be open in the sense that you are able to listen and share. Bernie Bickerstaff, coach of the Washington Wizards, understands how important it is to listen to your players. That's why he hired former Philadelphia Eagles cornerback John Outlaw as a full-time assistant—not because of Outlaw's basketball knowledge or teaching skills but because of his rapport with the players. Bickerstaff wanted somebody the players could talk to about anything.

A —— Awareness

You must understand the uniqueness of the individuals you are working with, and respect the potential that each one has. Phil Jackson of the Chicago Bulls likes to pick out books for his players to read on long road trips. He gears each book to the personality of the individual player. Math teacher Jaime Escalate, who was profiled in the movie *Stand and Deliver*, managed to motivate underprivileged high school students to pass the College Advanced Placement Mathematics Examination year after year. How? He saw their potential and found a way to uncover it.

C —— Commitment

Successful coaching is not a one-time encounter. It is a relationship built on trust and commitment. Whenever you find players voluntarily giving their best, you generally will find that coaches have earned the trust and the respect of the players. In addition to setting high standards, which most players want, coaches demonstrate their commitment to the players by:

- Respecting the dignity and worth of every player
- Asking for suggestions
- Providing long-term commitment to their goals, interests and needs
- Providing opportunities for them to develop and succeed
- Providing a quality learning environment
- Providing a reward system for all

H —— Honesty

You can't be helpful if you can't be truthful. For example, if you ask your players to be on time for practices, but you reward players who are late by giving them the same amount of game time or not criticizing them for their behavior, what message does that send to players who follow the rules? Beloved Colgate University basketball coach Jack Bruen, who coached right up until his death from cancer, once explained his own blunt honesty by saying he would tell you what you needed to hear and not what you wanted to hear. Consequently, his players always knew where they stood and what they needed to do in order to improve themselves.

As you can see, the manner in which you communicate with your players has great influence on them, and I'm not just talking about whether you yell at them or not. For example, how you respond to what your players do on the court has a greater influence on their thinking than what you tell them to do. Your response influences the development of their self-concept, attitude toward learning, achievement and rapport.

In other words, it's one thing to tell them to "think," but how do you respond when they do? Well or badly? There are two kinds of responses: those that close down communication between you and your players, and those that open it up. Closed responses include yelling, criticism, and meaningless praise. Open responses include using silence, accepting, and clarifying what they just said or did.

One mark of a good communicator is whether you have your team's ear. Do they listen to you? Do they respect you? Do they understand what you are teaching them? If they don't, then you need to be flexible enough to adapt your coaching/communicating style to better suit those you are working with.

Bernie Bickerstaff put it this way: "You have to understand that people are different, and different players respond to things in different ways, and you have to use whatever works to get your point across. If you know a guy doesn't respond to yelling, but he does to a calmer approach, then that's what you do to reach him."

Not all coaches agree with this, I know. P.J. Carlesimo, when confronted about the abrasive style that rubs so many of his players the wrong way, basically said, "Hey! I've been doing this for 27 years. I'm not about to change now." However, I believe that, while the student (or athlete) has a responsibility to learn, the teacher (or coach) has the responsibility to be an effective teacher. Sometimes that means altering or adjusting your style to reach the maximum number of individuals.

How you communicate with your players does more than just determine the kind of relationship you have with them. It also determines whether they will develop into athletes with court sense—including the ability to think for themselves on the court—or whether they will be nothing more than robots following the coach's directions.

COACHING FOR LEARNING

In a very real sense, they must teach themselves, and all we can do is provide every possible means to enable this self-instruction to take place.
                    - Robert Sternberg Ph.D., author of Successful Intelligence

Coaches inherit a learning situation that most teachers would envy. Unlike algebra or calculus class, the basketball court is a place where the kid WANTS to be. The subject is something they think is fun. They come motivated to learn because the subject is relevant and demands them to be engaged. With all that going for you, it would be a shame to use basketball as an avenue to teach nothing more than basketball.

WHY TEACH THINKING SKILLS?

It has been said that an educated person is someone who is equipped to identify and learn the lessons inherent in his or her various life experiences. Schools produce educated people by providing them with 1) the tools they need in order to learn from their experience, and 2) sample life experiences to practice their developing skills. Playing on a basketball team, for example, would fall into the category of a sample life experience. In order for that experience to be meaningful, the players have to first have the tools they need to learn from the experience. Now, of course, there will always be those extraordinary players who are able to take the analytical and problem-solving kind of thinking they learn in math class and put it to use on the basketball court. On the other hand, there are many more players who will never make the connection—unless you help them do it.

Coaches need to teach thinking. Why? Because some of these kids won't learn it anywhere else. Also, the need for thinking skills in order to succeed in the world is so great that every part of a child's learning should be concerned about it—even sports.

If we want to help kids develop the ability and the self-confidence to deal with problems and chart a life of their own choosing, we have to look at basketball as an opportunity to develop thinking skills. Roland Ortmayer, football coach at the University of La Verne in Southern California, is a staunch believer in having players do their own thinking. He refuses to have a play book or put coaches in the stands sending down plays. "If you do this, the coaches are just moving pawns and a few knights and castles. I want the game played by the people the game is for. We have 55 brains on the field. Think how foolish it would be not to use them all."

As Arthur Costa said, "The school will become a home for the mind only when the total school is an intellectually stimulating environment for all participants; when all the school's inhabitants realize that freeing human intellectual potential is the goal of education; when they strive to get better at it themselves; and when they use their energies to enhance the intelligent behavior of others."

SOME BASIC PRINCIPLES OF LEARNING

The issue of whether players should think while they're playing is a loaded one. However, if coaches want to encourage court sense in their players, they have to give them the freedom to think creatively.

If you don't want players to learn and develop, then never let them think for themselves. Tell them what to do rather than wait for them or help them figure out answers for themselves.

But if you do want your players to learn thinking skills as well as playing skills, then there are some basic principles of learning that you should be aware of:

- The more an athlete is involved (emotionally, interactively, leadership-wise), the more likely he or she is to learn and acquire useful information.

- All kids are intelligent in their own way. The challenge is to unlock or facilitate that intelligence.

- Different kids have different learning styles. Coaches must accommodate an array of thinking and learning styles, systematically varying teaching and assessment methods to reach every player.

The key is variety and flexibility. This doesn't mean you have to change your coaching style, but vary it. By doing this, you will find you have a lot more learners than you realized.

If a player is at all reflective about learning a new skill, they are mostly thinking about how they are doing in acquiring the skill—not how to use the skill. This is thinking at a low level; coaches need to encourage higher-level thinking.

What are some things you can do to encourage higher-level thinking in your players?

- Serve as a creative role model. Do you run the same old plays and drills, day in and day out? Or do you mix things up? Do you design creative drills?

- Encourage questioning of assumptions. Do your players assume that because you're the coach, you're always right? Or do they ever question what you say?

- Encourage sensible risk-taking, and allow your players to make mistakes when they do take risks.

- Let players define problems themselves. For example, instead of analyzing opponents for them, encourage them to do it. Instead of saying, "We play State tonight and here's what we are going to do," you could say, "We play State tonight. What do we know about them? What should we do?" Give them opportunities to exercise their thinking skills—analytical, creative, and practical. Share the coaching role with them.

- Reward creative ideas. Come up with a "Creative Play of the Week" contest.

- Allow time to think creatively. This can be challenging, because there's seldom enough time at practice to do all the things you need to do.

- Let your players know that creative thinkers often face obstacles (remember Bill Russell's story about how no one ever understood his constant desire to analyze the game?). They shouldn't feel discouraged if some of their ideas get shot down.

- Be sensitive to teaching opportunities and seize those opportunities to convey a message.

- Be willing to grow. Just because you've always done something one way doesn't mean you can't change or try something new.

- Recognize that creative thinkers need nurturing environments.

CREATING A NURTURING ENVIRONMENT FOR LEARNING

When you do things that help your players learn to use their higher-level thinking skills, you are creating a nurturing environment for learning. Learning is a consequence of thinking. So if you want your players to learn, they have to be able to think.

Author Peter Senge described a learning organization as one in which "people continually expand their capacity to create the results they truly desire, where new and expansive patterns of thinking are nurtured, where collective aspiration is set free, and where people are continually learning how to learn together." What I am trying to do is encourage coaches to create an environment that communicates loud and clear that athletes are fully capable of learning what they need for on- and off-court success—that the same principles of learning basketball apply to learning life skills.

The old model of coaching, in which the athlete is just supposed to do what the coach says, may yield short term results, but it hardly prepares the athlete to deal with situations where there is no coach to tell him what to do. It encourages players to conform to someone else's standards, rather than developing their own.

Teaching for thinking means creating conditions that are conducive to thinking. This means that:

(1) You pose problems and raise questions.

(2) You structure part of your practice time for thinking—value it and make time for it.

(3) You respond to players' ideas in such a way as to maintain a climate that creates trust, allows risk-taking, and is experimental, creative, and positive.

(4) You model the behaviors of thinking that are desired.

You can also help improve your players' thinking abilities by doing left brain/right brain activities. Basketball in particular and sports in general are intuitive and spontaneous activities that reinforce right brain functions. A more efficient learning environment can be created by utilizing:

- Verbal teaching of fundamentals and team drills for the left brain.
- Non-verbal teaching (demonstration of skills, walk-throughs of offenses and defenses, use of videotape and game review) for the right brain.

By getting both sides of the brain working, players can strengthen their game.

Coaches who promote a learning environment are coaches who stress academics. They ensure their players are doing well in school and monitor their progress. Many coaches also allow players to miss practices to prepare for exams or complete assignments that could not have been completed otherwise. Mike Krzyzewski of Duke felt academics were so important that he would not hang an NCAA championship banner in the Duke fieldhouse until all of the seniors on that team had graduated.

Court sense is a knowledge of the game, but more than that, it's retention of that knowledge and understanding of that knowledge, and most importantly, use of that knowledge. That's what you have to teach your players—not just the x's and o's of basketball. Knowledge includes skills, know-how, reflectiveness, and awareness of the issues as well as solutions to game situations. But your players aren't going to learn this unless you provide them with the right kind of environment.

Teaching something as complicated as court sense can be challenging. Psychologists have found that the human intellect has a limited capacity for handling variables—and teaching players court sense means teaching them to handle a lot of variables. Humans have the capacity for handling and coordinating on the average of seven different variables, decisions, or different pieces of information at one time. Give them any more than that, and they start to feel stressed. So just remember, a large part of creating a learning environment has to do with patience—on your part, and on the part of your kids.

COACHING FOR TRANSFER

If the processes don't transfer, they cannot even be called thinking. They can be called learning, memory or habit, but not thinking.
- Marilyn J. Adams

Athletes may need frequent reminders that, rather than being "just dumb jocks," they are multifaceted individuals who have demonstrated remarkable inner resources in their [sports] careers and who can learn to transfer their sports savvy to other fields of interest.
- Nancy Hilliard, coordinator of the
Career Assessment Program for Athletes

What is transfer? It is where something learned in one context helps you out in another. It's when you draw on past knowledge and apply it to new situations. In the past, the assumption in education has been that transfer takes care of itself. In other words, if you teach kids about chemical reactions in chemistry or physics, they will automatically "transfer" that knowledge to understand why their cake didn't rise in Home Ec. Well, guess what? Transfer does not take care of itself. If it did, you wouldn't have so many kids asking, "Why do I have to learn this? I'm never going to use it!"

You have to help the transfer process along. After all, there's little to be gained from knowledge used to pass a test or win a game if that knowledge can't be put to work in a person's daily life.

Athletes should be able to use what they learn in basketball to solve problems. Unless programs (including basketball programs) designed to teach thinking skills reflect the realities of everyday problem solving and decision making, it is doubtful that students will be able to apply what they have learned from these programs to their lives.

In your coaching, you can point out to athletes when they are using skills that transfer to real-world situations. As a role model for these and other skills, you can help your athletes think in job terms by identifying some of the skills you use: teaching, planning, leading, recruiting, analyzing, motivating, and disciplining, to name a few.

You can also help athletes recognize where sports skills will help them in other situations. For example, you could ask your players how the ability to play as a team and work with people you might not always like can help them in school or at home.

Getting the support of other school personnel can help with coaching for transfer. At Rancho Buena Vista High School in Vista, California, girls' basketball coach Kathy George instituted an Adopt-A-Player program. In this program, school personnel become on-campus "parents" for the athletes. The players' on-court achievements are supported by their "parents" through game attendance, personal posters, and good-luck salutations. The parents are also available to help with scholastic affairs. As one teacher said, "I really feel that the best way young ladies can learn how to handle themselves and be successful in the world is through team sports. Every single lesson they learn (in sports) is important."

Like other aspects of coaching court sense, coaching for transfer demands more work and effort on your part. But in the long run, what can be more rewarding than helping your athletes to develop skills on the court AND to capitalize on these assets in life's other challenges?

COACHING BY EXAMPLE

A life is not important except in the impact it has on other lives.
- Jackie Robinson

I don't know any other way to lead but by example.
- Don Shula, former NFL coach

If you're going to talk the talk, you've got to walk the walk. If you're going to talk about the importance of learning, you have to show that you are a learner. When athletes work with coaches who continue to see themselves as learners, who ask questions with which they themselves still grapple, who are willing and able to alter both content and practices in the pursuit of meaning, and who treat athletes and their endeavors as works in progress, not finished products, athletes are more likely to demonstrate these characteristics themselves.

Unlike most NBA coaches who only observe and evaluate summer league competition, Larry Bird chose to coach the Indiana Pacers' entry in the Atlanta Summer Shootout in 1997. "It's a chance for me to learn them and them to learn me," Bird said.

It was also a chance for Bird to show that he is a learner. As Pacers forward Dale David said, "His coaching here shows his dedication and willingness to learn."

We're at a point in time where student-athletes need more guidance than ever, because of the temptations that are out there. They see kids like Kobe Byrant being drafted out of high school, or they see others leaving college early to join the draft, and they think, "Hey, who needs education?" They need to have someone there to tell them why learning is important.

Almost anytime you see a kid from a deprived home who has managed to develop normally and rise above their circumstance, you can usually pinpoint someone in their lives who has been a caring, stimulating role model. That helps them rise above the mediocrity around them.

So be an example of someone who has a commitment to continued learning. To do that, you must ask yourself: Am I constantly observing objectively, evaluating and re-evaluating, or have I reached the point where I look, but am not aware of what I see?

COACHING THE SPECIFICS OF COURT SENSE

In the section on "How To Get Court Sense," I discussed seven specific things players need to learn in order to gain or improve their court sense. First and foremost, of course, was the importance of just learning how to learn. That was followed by the importance of learning the fundamentals, learning to be confident, learning to think the game, learning to work hard, learning to stay in control, and learning to develop character.

As a coach, if you want to encourage the development of court sense in your players, you need to be sure that your basketball program emphasizes each of these attributes.

TEACHING YOUR PLAYERS TO LEARN

Rockne liked smart and clever teams, and in his early coaching days, he found that he could not develop this trait on the field alone. There was not enough time. So he started a football lecture period, in a free class hour, immediately after lunch from one to one-forty. It was held daily throughout the regular football season and spring practice. During this forty minute period, football was turned upside down and inside out by Rockne. He was a remarkable teacher. His football lectures were classics, as his chemistry classes were classics. Other students who were not on his football squads would jam every available bit of space to hear him expound on the game.

- Harry A. Stuhldreher, *Knute Rockne: Man Builder*

The novice teacher shows and tells incessantly: the wise teacher listens, prods, challenges, and refuses to give the right answer. Ideally, the student remembers what they have learned, not what the teacher told them.

- from the teachings of Lao Tzu

Much of what you need to know in order to teach your players to learn, we already discussed in the section on "Coaching for Learning." However, since I believe you cannot over-emphasize the importance of using sports as a learning tool, let me just add a few more suggestions to what I've already said.

The first step to teaching your players to learn is to set the expectation by telling them again and again that you expect them to use their heads on and off the court. They might not believe you at first. The critical place where they will begin to believe you is when they make a mistake. You see, if you tell kids you want them to learn to think and they take you at your word, they will make mistakes. If you give them a supportive response, then they won't be afraid to try the next time.

To help your players learn, you have to understand their point of view. Most of us think of a coach as someone who talks and passes information to someone else. But you also have to listen. That means giving players opportunities to express their point of view. It includes asking them to elaborate on their thinking. For example, one player on the Stanford women's basketball team was notorious for stopping practice to ask questions. Coach Tara VanDerveer said, "That's one of the advantages of coaching at Stanford. You have smart players. I see stopping practice like that as thinking, not challenging my authority. I encourage them to think. I tell them flat out: 'If you're depending on me to do all your thinking, you're in trouble...'"

Robert Sternberg has said: "I believe that the single most helpful thing we can do to help children develop their intelligence is a simple one: take their questions seriously, and turn those questions into golden opportunities to think and learn."

Your goal is to have players who can behave intelligently on the court. There are several characteristics of intelligent behaviors. Some of these include:

- Persistence
- Decreasing impulsivity
- Listening to others and thinking cooperatively
- Flexible thinking
- Metacognition, or awareness of your own thinking
- Striving for accuracy and precision
- Questioning and problem posing
- Risk taking
- Creativity
- Enjoyment of problem solving

What can you do to encourage these attitudes and actions in your players? Take metacognition, for example. Making players more aware of their own thinking processes can be as simple as saying, "That was a great play! What made you think of doing that?"

TEACHING YOUR PLAYERS THE FUNDAMENTALS

The key to developing people is to catch them doing something right.
- Ken Blanchard and Spencer Johnson, The One Minute Manager

Improving Your Effectiveness as a Coach

Every coach agrees that the fundamentals of basketball are critical. However, does this belief translate to what you do as a coach? Do you give it lip service or do you really believe it?

After reading through countless books on basketball, talking to coaches, looking at clinic agendas, I can see that very little time is spent on fundamentals. When the subject is addressed, it usually lacks details.

There is also a widespread attitude that fundamentals are for little kids, and that by the time players are in high school or college, they should know all that stuff. Well, maybe they should, but it's obvious they don't! Just look at the free-throw statistics in the NBA. The NBA's foul-shot percentage has always been between 63 percent and 78 percent. Why is it so low? After all, in the NBA you have the best players, who also have plenty of time to practice. Playing basketball is their full-time job. So why aren't they better at it? The answer lies in poor fundamentals.

If your players practice shooting 200 shots a day but really only pay attention to about 50 of those shots, then they're wasting 150 shots. In fact, 150 semiconscious shots may be doing them more harm than good. Why? Because you can form bad habits without noticing it. As a coach, you must help your players become more aware of what they are doing. Remind them that practice doesn't make perfect—only perfect practice makes perfect.

Former Miami Dolphins coach Don Shula suggests a five-step plan for reducing practice errors:

(1) Tell people what you want them to do.
(2) Show them what good performance looks like.
(3) Let them do it.
(4) Observe their performance.
(5) Praise progress and/or redirect.

Using Shula's plan, here is how I would teach my players how to screen and roll. First, I would explain what a screen and roll is. Then I would demonstrate the process of screening and rolling. Next, I would ask each player, in their own words, to describe how to screen and roll, and then I would have them pair off and demonstrate the skill. As each pair completed their demonstration, I would have the other players critique and encourage them. I would then offer my evaluation.

Coaches spend too much time on teaching plays and not enough time on fundamentals. Teach your players the fundamentals and they will make the plays. As a player, you can't learn how to make adjustments for every situation by practicing pre-designed plays. You have to have the fundamentals that allow you to creatively respond in game situations. The fundamentals are the building blocks of learning court sense.

TEACHING YOUR PLAYERS CONFIDENCE

The primary reason to have a coach is to have somebody who can look at you and say, "Man, you're lookin' good today."
- Jack Daniels

Coming up with confidence-building experiences for kids can be a challenge. These experiences need to be doable for the athlete, and yet challenging enough to encourage growth. The differences that exist in the ability of people to cope successfully with stressful situations are learned primarily during childhood and adolescent years. Athletics can be an important arena in which such skills are learned. The athletic experience can be a laboratory for trying out and mastering ways of dealing with stress.

As a coach, you are in a position to help your young athletes develop the skills that make up mental toughness. Most sports stress results from one of two things: 1) fear of getting hurt and 2) fear of failure (or looking really, really, stupid). To deal with the first fear, you improve their skills. To deal with the second fear is more challenging. The ideas that underlie the fear of failure do not arise in a vacuum. They almost always have been communicated to youngsters by their parents or other important adults, including coaches. The fastest way to create fear of failure is to punish unsuccessful performance by criticizing it or by withholding approval.

You can have a dramatic impact in helping the young athlete develop a positive desire to achieve rather than a fear of failure. Here are some ways you can do this:

Improving Your Effectiveness as a Coach

(1) **Reduce situational stress**. Use encouragement and reinforcement to strengthen desirable behaviors. This develops a positive desire to achieve and succeed rather than a negative fear of making mistakes. This lets athletes see successful performance as an opportunity to experience a reward, rather than a way of avoiding punishment.

(2) **Increase the athlete's resources**. We feel insecure when we don't have the skills needed to cope with a situation. Many young athletes experience this insecurity when they first begin to learn a sport. Thus, improving their skills is one way you can help to reduce athletic stress. Competence is always a precursor to confidence.

(3) **Develop winning attitudes toward competition**. There is a big difference between pressure situations and feeling pressure. Mentally tough athletes perform well in pressure situations because they have eliminated the pressure. There's no way to eliminate pressure situations; they will always be there because they are a part of competition. But you don't have to let them psyche you out. Mentally tough athletes think like this:

- I'm going to do the best I can and let the cards fall where they may.
- This is supposed to be fun, and I'm going to make sure it is.
- I'm going to focus on the good things that will happen when I make the play.
- I'm concentrating on performing, rather than winning or losing.

(4) **Introduce pressure situations into practice**. One of the greatest fears for most athletes is that they will choke under pressure. So introduce them to shooting contests, last-minute situations where the game is on the line, free throws late in practice when everyone is tired and when missing a free throw has consequences.

(5) **To help foster confidence, you must also foster courage**. That courage includes creative courage, which comes from asking questions and trying new things. Asking questions and challenging the established order of things is part of education, but it is antithetical to most sports subcultures. For many coaches, questioners are quickly

labeled as troublemakers whose ideas must be silenced lest the coach's authority be challenged.

As a coach, the attitude you communicate to your players has a lot to do with how confident they feel and how well they handle pressure. Here are some specific attitudes that can and should be communicated to players by a coach:

- Sports should be fun.
- Anything worth achieving is rarely easy.
- Mistakes are a necessary part of learning anything well.
- Effort is what counts.
- Do not confuse worth with performance (what you do is not what you are).
- Pressure is something you put on yourself.
- Try to like and respect your opponents.

Some coaches do not know how to use good performances and winning efforts as confidence builders. A common belief among coaches is that too much success can lead to complacency. So they play down individual and team achievements and remind the players how much more they have to learn. You read comments like this all the time in the sports pages: "Yeah, we won, but we have a lot of room for improvement." Rarer, but more valuable, are comments like this: "It was disappointing to lose, but I'm proud of the effort my team made."

When Rick Pitino coached Kentucky, he tried this confidence booster on one of his players. He knew the player read the sports section of the local newspaper faithfully. So every time Pitino saw a reporter, he talked excitedly about the player's improvement and how much the team needed him. The player's confidence shot up when he read the things the coach was saying about him. The trick worked, and the player went on to a successful career at Kentucky.

TEACHING YOUR PLAYERS TO THINK THE GAME

I want these players to intellectualize the game.

- Pete Newell

Pete Newell has been it all: coach of an NIT champion, an NCAA champion, and an Olympic champion; general manager of the Los Angeles Lakers; member of the Basketball Hall of Fame; and the force behind Pete Newell's Big Man Camp, which has taught nearly 100 current and countless former NBA giants. He knows basketball. Even more, he knows how to coach basketball players. When Newell teaches, he never resorts to making fun of his players or yelling at them. Instead, he challenges them to think the game. A player's question is usually met by a question from Newell, forcing the player to come up with an answer of his or her own. Newell is never happier than when a player takes something that Newell taught and improves upon it.

Thinking the game is one of the hardest things to try to teach your players, but one of the most rewarding things is when you see them "getting it." Here are some strategies that I and others have used to help players learn how to think the game.

Teach them to play without the ball.

One of the most difficult coaching tasks is to teach a player to carry out actions that don't involve the basketball. Some points to emphasize to your players:

- Be alert. Use the entire floor to your advantage when beginning a move.
- Move with authority, balance, and quickness.
- Move with purpose.
- Read the defense and the ball, then respond.
- Get open or get out of the way—don't just stand still.
- Know and use the perfect receiving position for receiving the ball.
- Be a good actor (use good fakes, take the initiative).
- Lose the defender.
- Get close to get open.
- Set strong, noisy and legal screens.
- Set picks or screens at right angles to the expected path of the defender.

Encourage players to think by using "thinking" words when you talk to them.

For example:

- Let's look at these two plays.
- Let's compare these two plays.

- What do you think will happen when...?
- What do you predict will happen when...?

- What do you think would have happened if...?
- What do you speculate would have happened if...?

- How else could you use this...?
- How could you apply this...?

Use huddles effectively.

A coach can stop play during practice and huddle with his players to make an important point about understanding the game. For example, a coach is working on the team's delay game in practice. He stops practice, huddles the players and explains the why's of what they are doing, or points out specifics that require thinking (fake before you pass, allow a jump ball to occur rather than make a bad pass, etc.). The huddle changes the learning modality from action reflection.

In my work as an organizational and management consultant, I often suggest that managers call huddles with their staff to make a point or call attention to a need. This means that the group literally huddles around the manager to deal with the issue. Because they are standing no one fears a long and unproductive meeting. This makes them more attentive to what is being said.

Find time for one-on-one conversations.

Another teaching tactic is for the coach and player to meet somewhere for a comfortable conversation about specific aspects of the thinking part of the game. Use this time to talk about the why's and why not's of certain offensives, defensives, and specific aspects of the player's game. There are many things that have to do with the game that don't show up on the stat sheet that are really hard to explain, but are all part of court sense. Examples of court sense can be shared and discussed.

Be aware of the little things.

My friend Dave Bollwinkel uses various tactics to try to teach his players to think the game. For example, to make players aware of just how much time they have when the 10-second clock or the 35-second clock begins to run, Dave has his players stand behind the inbound line, close their eyes, and count to 10. When they get to 10, they are to jump forward across the line. Dave said it's amazing how many jump too soon.

Dave also gets his bench involved in helping players on the floor take maximum advantage of the details that can spell the difference between winning and losing games. For example, the entire bench stands as soon as the 10-second shot count starts, as well as whenever the coach calls for a time-out. During time-outs, each person on the bench stands behind his counterpart on the floor to better understand the coach's advice to him.

Dave also advises his players to let the referee know when they are going to foul an opponent, so the ref can waste as little time as possible in making the call. He also tells his players to always ask the officials if the situation allows the team to run the baseline when try-ing to inbound the ball (some situations do, others don't).

Teach players to think on the run.

Dave likes to help his players learn to think on the run by having players running different drills at each end of the court. When he blows his whistle, they must change drills before he can run to the other end of the court. During the time it takes him to run the court, they must exercise enough leadership and teamwork to get organized and begin running the particular drill suggested by his whistle.

The mother of tennis champ Martina Hingis (who served as her daughter's coach) used a similar strategy. She used to hit balls all over the court to keep Martina's notoriously short attention span from wan-dering and to encourage her to think on the court. Hingis' head for strategy seems a direct result of her mother's desire to instill indepen-dent thought. Hingis really isn't that athletic, but she is an incredible thinker, and an incredible tennis player.

TEACHING YOUR PLAYERS TO WORK HARD

Ambition by itself never gets anywhere until it forms a partnership with hard work.

-James Garfield

Success is sweet, but it usually has the scent of sweat about it.

-Anonymous

If I don't practice for one day, I know it, if I don't practice for two days, the CRITICS know it, if I don't practice for three days, EVERYONE knows it.

- Ignance Paderewski, the great Polish pianist

The will to win is not nearly as important as the will to prepare to win.

- Anonymous

One of the most boring, tedious things for any athlete to do is the conditioning involved in staying in shape. Playing the game is fun; lifting weights or running sprints is not. Neither is practicing the end-less drills and repetitions that are so critical to learning the basic skills of basketball. So how do you help your athletes learn the importance of doing these things?

First, you need to make sure your players really understand the need for conditioning. We sort of take it for granted that they do, because as adults we've been bombarded for years with information about diet and exercise. But kids aren't always aware of all this stuff— or else they think it applies to everyone else, but not them.

Conditioning gets the body ready for the physical and mental de-mands of sport. The body needs to be warmed-up and, ideally, the specific muscles should be stretched before and after a workout. While you want your players to be in good condition, you have to be careful about having them over-train. I have seen coaches go nuts in this area as they try to use conditioning as a tool to weed out the weak or establish discipline. Sometimes they will make their team run for hours, or do all sorts of exercises that have little or nothing to do with the demands of their specific sport. As a result, the majority of the practice time is wasted.

"Specificity" is a training principle with which all physical educators and fitness specialists are familiar. This means the training for the sport should match the physical demands of the activity. Only then can the training be transferred to the sport. If you are engaged in a sport like basketball, which requires quickness and endurance, the conditioning program should match those demands. Because basketball involves a lot of running, jumping, and short sprinting, conditioning should emphasize jump training, leg strength, spirit training and anaerobic interval work. Conditioning drills should be based on the fundamentals of movement, dribbling, and defense.

However, a lot of young coaches make their teams run for long distances out on the track. I remember those runs. Now I know that we were training our muscles in the wrong way. Running distances will break down the fast twitch muscle fibers in the body and thus decrease a person's jump and speed.

To encourage conditioning, be generous with your reinforcement, as well as specific and concrete about the things you say and instructions you give. Have realistic expectations as well as consistency in rewarding and reinforcing achievement. Remember that it is just as important to reward effort as it is to reward successful outcomes.

Don't overlook the importance of desire as a motivator. I'm sure you're familiar with the *Rocky* movies. In *Rocky*, Rocky Balboa had the goal of going 15 rounds with the champion. He didn't win the fight, but he reached his goal and won personal and public respect. In *Rocky II*, Rocky's goal was to win the world championship. He won. In *Rocky III*, Rocky lost his crown because he lost sight of his goal. He forgot his priorities. He wasn't hungry anymore. That's when Apollo Creed, Rocky's one-time foe, challenged him to find the eye of the tiger. Creed took Rocky back to his beginnings—to the sweaty, dirty, cramped gym that he used to work in. Rocky found the eye of the tiger. He got hungry again and regained his world championship.

143

Desire is the best motivator for working hard. Remind your players that if you want success, you have to pay the price. Help them set personal and team goals. Show them how to measure their progress by achieving short-term goals on the way to a long-term goal.

Finally, be an example to your players of someone who believes in the importance of physical fitness, hard work, and preparation. During his tenure as coach of the Miami Dolphins, Don Shula said, "My own preparation for every game has to be exemplary. I am dedicated to success and will do whatever it takes to achieve it. I am generally the last one off the practice field."

TEACHING YOUR PLAYERS TO STAY IN CONTROL

The first, and most crucial aspect of teaching your players self-control is to model it yourself. There are two funny scenes in Penny Marshall's movie, *A League of Their Own*, that illustrate how a coach's ability (or lack of ability) to stay in control can influence his or her players. In the first scene, Tom Hanks plays the manager of a women's baseball team who chews out one of his players for missing the cutoff on a throw from the outfield. As he rages, the player begins to cry. Hanks gets angrier and angrier, saying, "There's no crying in baseball!" Later in the season, the player makes the same mistake. This time Hanks' character has learned a lot. With great physical effort, he remains calm (for him) and suggests that the player continue to work on the skill. She responds well to his disciplined, positive approach and comes through with a big play in the final game.

If you have gotten away with having a short fuse in other areas of your life, you will definitely not get away with it for long when you coach young athletes. You must learn to take things in stride and continually remind yourself why you are coaching. However, even the most even-tempered coach in the world gets tested. I have seen the calmest and most serene people kick balls, throw clipboards, break pencils—in other words, totally lose it. The key is to let out your frustrations a little at a time, in a respectable manner.

You can also help athletes learn self-control by teaching them how to control stress with relaxation techniques. These include such things as deep breathing, muscle relaxation, centering, visualization, autogenic training, and coping affirmations.

If an athlete doesn't seem to recognize his or her own "hot buttons," then you point them out. Learning to control your emotions involves understanding what situations pressure you, what happens to you when you become anxious, and what coping responses will help.

Behavioralists know that behavior that is rewarded is more likely to occur again. Behavior that goes unreinforced is eventually extinguished. When your players show self-control, reward them for it. Letting learners know that they have modified their behavior toward a desired outcome serves as a reinforcement.

Players who know their coach cares about them and how they act are also more likely to exhibit self-control. In 1958, an explosive shot-putter at the University of California—a giant of a man who stood 6'5"—blew up at a meet when an official ruled one of his throws a foul. The previous fall, this same athlete had been a member of the football team, but in a moment of temper, busted one of his teammates on the chin and knocked him out. Not surprisingly, the coach threw him off the team. This time, however, the athlete quickly realized the seriousness of his outburst and retreated to the shot-putter's bench. After the meet, reporters asked the coach if the athlete would get the boot again? The coach replied, "Why, of course not ... A coach's job is to help his boys, help them in every way possible. How could I help this boy if he is not on the squad?"

Later, the athlete in question explained how the coach helped him with his problem temper:

> He never bawled me out. He never sweet-talked me. Rather, there was just something about him that told me he cared about me. He was the first person who ever did. I knew he understood my problems. And brother, I had them. I was really hurt when I was kicked off the football squad. I wanted to bust something again. But soon I had become so fond of Brutus (Hamilton, the coach) that I couldn't do anything bad. I knew it would hurt him. I was going to bust that track official. But just then I thought of Brutus. It would have been like hitting him.

I guess he taught me...by example. No matter what happened, Brutus never lost his poise. He always conducted himself like a gentleman. He always said the right things. I found myself wanting to be like him.

One reason we try to teach players confidence and mental toughness is because the athlete who is mentally tough is an athlete who can exercise self-control. So if you're having problems with an athlete or athletes who keep blowing (or imploding) at inopportune times, then it's quite likely you're looking at a self-esteem problem. Try improving the athlete's self-confidence, and I'll bet you'll see improvement in self-control.

TEACHING YOUR PLAYERS CHARACTER

When the player's basketball career has run its course, what has the player gained from sports? All involved—players, parents, coaches, and teachers—hope the experiences, relationships, and habits developed through participation in a well-managed sports program will have provided the athlete the opportunity to develop sound habits and attitudes that will help them become good citizens and good people. The "best" coaches are those who have succeeded in establishing that triple goal: a good basketball program, a good basketball team, and good people.

- Gregory A. Marsh, "Coaching Character...Both 'Talkin' and Walkin': The Role of the Coach in Developing Character in Players" (independent research project)

I sincerely hope that no coach reading this book subscribes to the belief that it's a coach's job to teach basketball—period. But if you do feel the need to ask the question "Why should a basketball coach be expected to teach values?" let me just answer: Because the best coaches do.

Being a person of strong, moral character is part of being a complete player, and definitely part of being a complete person. I believe that athletics can help develop character, that coaches influence their players, and that coaches can play a positive role in developing character in their players. Mere participation in sport is not what builds character in athletes. Rather, it is how that sport is conducted—in other words, the role of the coach.

That doesn't mean you have to tell your players what to believe. Rather, it means laying the groundwork so that they can think for themselves and make educated choices based on a set of fundamental, or core, values. The Marine Corps discovered it had to begin educating recruits about fundamental values after 22 Marines were implicated in the Tailhook scandal and a pair were found guilty in the 1995 rape of an Okinawan school girl. Drill instructors now have long talks on morality and choices. "We're teaching them how to think, rather than telling them what to think," said a staff sergeant.

What can you do to help your players develop character?

(1) **Be there for them**. If your players know you are concerned and will protect them, it instills trust. People who are most willing to do the right thing have had the right thing done to them.

(2) **Live the right values**. It's not what you say, it's how you live. Treat your players the way you want them to treat others: fairly, honestly, and with justice.

(3) **Instill self-esteem**. The more you can make your players feel that they are worthwhile, the more they will be willing to do good to others.

As a coach, you have to realize that you are more than just someone who teaches sports. You are a leader. Youth are highly impressionable, particularly in the field of sports. Whether you realize it or not, whether you want to be or not, you are a hero to many. That means you have a responsibility to make an impact.

Frank McGuire, a former head basketball coach and member of the Basketball Hall of Fame, said, "All coaches teach character—and their degree of success is in no way measured by games won or lost. Most important of all, the coach must remember that he represents the type of[person] to whom he would entrust his own[child] for character training."

What values should you teach as a coach? That is for you to decide. It is important for you to reflect about which values you think are most important. If the values you represent as important to your team are truly important to you, you will be more likely to instill them in others. In his book, *They Call Me Coach*, John Wooden wrote about several values or qualities that he considered important to both basketball and life success. These included: ambition, adaptability, resourcefulness, fight (effort and hustle), sincerity, honesty, integrity, reliability, patience, and faith.

Some coaches tailor specific basketball drills during practice to bring out the values they think are important for good basketball players to have. With these types of drills, coaches can reinforce a variety of values, such as confidence, hard work, persistence, and teamwork. There are also many chances to stress these same qualities in situations off the court.

Greg Marsh noted in his research on coaching character: "One college coach values team unity—the idea that no one individual is more important than the team, and a sensitivity toward others rather than selfishness. That coach also wants to foster a sense of responsibility in his players. Each year, prior to the first away game, he announces to the team that the bus will leave at a precise time and suggests that they arrive at the bus a few minutes early. The coach makes a point to board the bus at exactly the appointed minute, takes his seat at the front, and tells the driver to go. All this is done without ever taking a roll call of players or even turning his head to see who is on the bus. Usually, he leaves at least one player behind on that first trip, sometimes a starter, sometimes a substitute. But he makes his point quite effectively—no one is ever late for the next trip!"

Players on the Utah Jazz team quickly learn that when coach Jerry Sloan tells them to be someplace by a certain time, it's best to show up five or 10 minutes early. They've gotten so good at this that sometimes the team bus even leaves ahead of schedule, simply because all the players are already there. Not so coincidentally, the Jazz also have a reputation for being responsible, team-oriented players.

One basketball coach doesn't have team rules. Rather, he has a list of "expectations." This allows the coach to state his values and reinforce the idea of a team built on mutual trust in fulfilling expectations, rather than developing an adversarial relationship. Another coach allows his team to come up with team rules, putting the responsibility on them to determine how they should behave.

Winning and building character don't have to be two opposing forces. If a coach is successful at teaching those attributes that make a good basketball player, he will also develop good people because the virtues are so similar.

The key to balancing teaching and competition is how you define success. If you define success as the self-satisfaction of knowing you have done your best, then you can lose games—even lose seasons—and still be a winner.

A TEACHER AND A COACH

Throughout this section, I have used the words "teach" and "coach" almost interchangeably. If you haven't already, then you must accept the idea that you are a teacher as well as a coach. You are an introducer of ideas, as well as a developer of player and person. You are there to teach ideas, not just skills. By doing so, you will do far more than develop players with court sense and basketball ability. You will develop individuals with the tools to succeed in life.

PART FOUR

FROM COURT SENSE
TO LIFE SENSE

Chapter 10

PLAYING THE TRANSITION GAME

The most interesting thing about Bill Bradley was not just that he was a great basketball player, but that he succeeded so amply in other things that he was doing at the same time, reached a more promising level of attainment, and, in the end, put basketball aside because he had something better to do.

        - John McPhee, *A Sense of Where You Are*

One of the books I came across while doing the research for this one was a wonderful little book by John McPhee called *A Sense of Where You Are*. In it, McPhee follows the college career of one of basketball's greatest players—Bill Bradley. For those of you who might not be familiar with Bradley's history, let me briefly recount it.

Bill Bradley was a highly recruited high school player who ignored all the scholarship offers thrown his way and instead decided to play for Princeton University—a school that didn't offer athletic scholarships. While at Princeton, he broke just about every basketball record there was to break. After graduation, Bradley passed on the opportunity to immediately turn pro and instead accepted a Rhodes Scholarship to study in Oxford, England. Upon returning to the United States, Bradley joined the New York Knicks. He played for the Knicks for 10 years, helping them win two championships along the way. When Bradley left the Knicks, he immediately threw his energy and talents into politics. He became one of the most well-respected members of the U.S. Senate, and his name has often been spoken of in terms of running for presidential office.

Not bad for a guy who once claimed he didn't "have that much natural ability" when it came to playing basketball. But what Bill Bradley did have was the ability and desire to develop his court sense, and to carry that sense with him even after he left the basketball court.

Remember the things we said about court sense? They include the ability to understand the game, to "get the big picture" on the court, to make good decisions, and to be a team player. Bradley had all of these things. For example, he was such a team player that the coach often had to tell him to stop passing so much and shoot more. He was so good at seeing the court that during the course of writing *A Sense of Where You Are*, McPhee took Bradley to an eye doctor to have his vision tested. As it turned out, Bradley did have better-than-average peripheral vision.

Of course, just because you can see all the players on the court doesn't mean you know what to do with them. That's where understanding the game and making good decisions comes in. Those qualities are not something you are born with—you have to learn them. I remember when I played basketball, I could not only see where everyone was on the court, but I knew where they had been and where they were going. Bradley was the same way. He was able to make spectacular passes because he thought ahead. If a player was at a certain point on the floor, Bradley would pass to where that player should be if he kept on going the way he should go.

Bill Bradley worked hard to learn and understand every nuance of the game. As McPhee wrote: "Because Bradley's inclination to analyze every gesture in basketball is fairly uncommon, other players look at him as if they think him a little odd when he seeks them out after a game and asks them to show him what they did in making a move that he particularly admired ...." Bradley told me about this almost apologetically, explaining that he had no choice but to be analytical in order to be in the game at all.

For Bradley, no detail was too small to be overlooked. Remember when we talked about knowing your environment? I know there are probably some readers who thought, "Does it really matter whether the basket is mobile or retractable?" The answer is yes, it does. Little things do matter. For example, when the floor of the Princeton gym was being resurfaced, Bradley had to practice at another gym.

McPhee went along to watch. The first afternoon, Bradley began by shooting jump shots from the right side. For some reason, he kept missing them. Finally, he stopped, made what appeared to McPhee to be "a mental adjustment," and then went on to hit several in a row. Then Bradley commented, "That basket is about an inch and a half low." A few weeks later, McPhee went back to measure the basket. It was one and one-eighth inches too low.

When it came to basketball, Bill Bradley worked hard . . . period. In high school, Bradley practiced three and a half hours every day after school, 9 to 5 on Saturday, and 1:30 to 5 on Sunday. In the summer, he would practice about three hours a day. McPhee said that Bradley "put ten pounds of lead slivers in his sneakers, set up chairs as opponents and dribbled in slalom fashion around them, and wore eyeglass frames that had a piece of cardboard taped to them so that he could not see the floor, for a good dribbler never looks at the ball."

Now the thing that I really admire about Bill Bradley was that he recognized he could use the things he learned playing basketball to help him achieve success in other areas. "Basketball discipline carries over into your life," he often told people. That discipline helped him to be a hard worker and a good student. It helped him not to waste his off-seasons as a professional, but to use them in working for such organizations as the Office of Economic Opportunity in Washington, D.C., and the Urban League street academies in Harlem. The things Bradley learned about being a team player helped him as he began gathering support for his senatorial campaign and, later, as he worked to get various pieces of legislation passed. What he learned about seeing the big picture helped him understand that he wouldn't always be playing basketball.

John McPhee wrote: "The metaphor of basketball is to be found in these compounding alternatives. Every time a basketball player takes a step, an entire new geometry of action is created around him. In 10 seconds, with or without the ball, a good player may see perhaps a hundred alternatives and, from them, make a half dozen choices as he goes along. A great player will see even more alternatives and will make more choices, and this multiradial way of looking at things will carry over into his life." That pretty much sums up what court sense can do for you and why it's such an important quality to develop. Having court sense gives you more choices—in basketball and in life.

COURT SENSE OFF THE COURT

I try to teach the kids that being successful has to be more than ending with a win. There's more to football than that. It's about applying all the things you learn in the game ... consistency, getting up after you get knocked down, working with and caring for other people, loyalty to each other, humility, all of it ... to life itself.

- Tom Larson, high school football coach

Going away 500 miles for a hometown guy, a city boy, to a place where there are only 22,000 people in the whole community, it was hard to make that transition. I was young, 17, and not ready to take the challenge of being a college student.

- Donnie Ellison, Washington State point guard

In basketball, each game is a problem to be solved. When you work to develop your court sense, you become a better problem solver. You sharpen your ability to identify the problem, come up with solutions, and carry out those solutions. In more technical terms, you put to work that analytical, creative, and practical intelligence that we talked about in the beginning of this book.

But that's not all. The great thing about court sense is that it comes with a "buy one-get one free" offer. It's not just for use on the basketball court. You can use your court sense skills just about anywhere. You can use them in the classroom. You can use them at work. You can use them in your relationships with other people.

There is a catch, though. The court sense you use in sports doesn't automatically follow you everywhere you go. It's up to you to figure out how to put what you've learned to use.

Every good team, every good player, is adept at transitioning from offense to defense and vice-versa. Now I want to talk about another transition game—the transferring of the thinking skills you learn on the court to your other activities. Transitioning involves flexibility and quick thinking. These are skills that are as valuable in everyday life as they are in basketball.

Making the transition from "basketball sense" to "life sense" involves other skills as well. You need to learn how to reflect on your experiences, put them into a positive framework, become a more self-aware person, and leverage, or make the most of, what you know about yourself and your abilities.

REFLECTING ON YOUR EXPERIENCES

Don't assume that because you are a successful team player on your basketball team you will automatically know how to be a successful team player in your family or at your job or on your debate squad. Before that can happen, you have to consciously think about what kinds of things you do in the game that make you a team player—like not being selfish, encouraging your teammates, and doing things to make others look good. Then you have to think about how you can do those things off the court.

Making an effort to understand what has happened to you and what it means is called reflecting. Reflecting means regularly taking time to think about things that happen to you in your daily life, and figuring out how they apply to your long-term dreams and goals.

Great people always take time to reflect on their lives. Gandhi took daily walks, meditated, and engaged in regular strategy sessions with his closest associates. Mozart showed his capacity for reflection in the many letters he wrote to family members. Often these letters included discussions of musical problems or challenges he was facing. Freud from an early age was constantly involved in thinking about his goals and the success or failure he was encountering. We need to be able to reflect in order to learn from our experiences.

FRAMING YOUR EXPERIENCES

In the middle of difficulty lies opportunity.

- Albert Einstein

Every day each of us encounters some experiences that go well and some that don't. Extraordinary people have the capacity to learn from bad experiences. They can take what others might think is an experience to forget as quickly as possible and instead reflect on it, think it over, and use the information they come up with to do things differently in the future.

Athletes do this all the time when they play sports. Let's say your team gets blown out by an opponent. What does the coach do? Ignore the game and pretend it never happened? Hardly. Instead, he or she points out the areas where the team made mistakes, and recommends ways to improve the next time you play.

"Framing" is the ability to put a negative experience in a positive light. That doesn't mean we enjoyed the experience or want to go through it again. Rather, framing allows us to find meaning in negative experiences. Without that meaning, many of life's experiences would simply be too hard to bear.

Let me give you a real-life example. A man, his wife, their four children, and two other family members were returning from the wedding of the man's youngest sister. As their two vehicles approached the freeway on-ramp, a drunken driver mistakenly exited the ramp and plowed head-on into the first vehicle. In the resulting accident, several people were injured and the couple's youngest daughter, who was only three years old, was killed.

As the family struggled to cope with this devastating and senseless loss, they discovered many "miracles" that helped them find meaning in disaster. Apparently, the drunk driver had sideswiped two vehicles before the collision. If that hadn't happened, he probably would have killed all of them. In addition, shortly before the accident occurred, the man had passed his wife's vehicle (a van) and taken the lead with his sturdier pick-up. If he hadn't done that, everyone in the van would have been killed. The young father also found meaning in the fact that, not long before the accident happened, his little girl had awakened, hugged his arm, and said, "I love you, Daddy." He was able to tell her that he loved her, too. The knowledge that these were their last words to each other was a great comfort to him.

There may come a time when you lose a scholarship or a job or a loved one, and you feel like it's the worst thing that will ever happen to you. This is when you take that experience and put it in a more positive "frame" by finding a way to learn or grow from it.

Playing the Transition Game

BECOMING SELF-AWARE

All of the significant battles are waged within the self.

- Sheldon Lopp

Self-awareness is an important part of your personal development. You can't live up to your basketball or life potential without understanding yourself.

Effective people know themselves. People with greater certainty about themselves are better pilots of their own lives.

The problem is, we would just as soon ignore our own weaknesses, or blame them on someone else. We fight self-awareness (life's little wake-up calls) by hitting our internal snooze alarm. We stay asleep. We stay in our comfort zone.

Awareness is a choice. Some people choose to sleepwalk through class, sports, relationships, careers, and other life experiences. Others choose to be aware of what their strengths and weaknesses are, and where they need to make changes in order to improve themselves.

If you think about the role models or mentors in your life, they are usually people who have a strong sense of who they are and what's important to them. They know what they believe in, they know what they want, and they know what they need to do to get it. They are generally those who make positive things happen.

If you would like to try getting to know yourself a little better, here are some questions to ask:

(1) What people, activities, or things are important to me?
(2) What do I like to do when I can do anything I want?
(3) What do I enjoy sharing with others?
(4) Is there anything I haven't done but I really, really want to do?
(5) What am I doing during the moments when I feel happiest and at peace with myself?
(6) To what am I willing to dedicate my life?
(7) Which of the above reflects what I really want, not just what I think I should do or what others may want me to do?

LEVERAGING YOURSELF

What does it mean to leverage yourself? Leveraging means using your strengths to gain a competitive advantage. This is what Jeff Hornacek did when he concentrated on becoming a player who could make the difficult shots. He knew he would never be the tallest or the strongest or the fastest, so he found an area where he could be the best and he developed that area.

What are your strengths? Maybe you're a "people" person — the one that cheers everyone else up after a bad game. Maybe you're a good decision-maker. Or maybe you're the one who always stays cool under pressure. While you want to develop all your skills, you also want to look for those things you are especially good at, and make them better. That's how you increase your value.

Now, how can you leverage your basketball skills to help you get ahead in other areas? Let's use the dreaded college application as an example. Most of them require that you answer at least one essay question. Let's say the question is, "Why do you think you should be admitted to State University?" If you were known as the hardest-working player on the team, you might answer: "Even though I began as a lowly third-string player, I put in more practice hours than anyone else. I spent hours reading about basketball and studying games. Eventually, I worked my way up to varsity. This taught me how to work hard for something I really want. You may have a lot of students who are smarter than I am, but you'll never have one who will work harder to succeed."

Businesses practice leveraging all the time. How often have you seen a product come out that says "new and improved"? What the company is doing is hoping that the good reputation of the old product will make you want to buy the new one. Or sometimes a company will bring out an entirely new product, and, in their advertisements, they'll say, "Brought to you by the same company that makes such-and-such." In this case, the company is hoping that if you believe they're competent enough to make a good stereo, they'll be competent enough to make a good television set.

Hollywood is nothing but one big leveraging game. For example, a director has a movie he really wants to make, but he doesn't have the money. So he gets some big-name stars interested, and then he goes to the studio and says, "If you give me the money to make this movie, I can guarantee Jack Nicholson for the lead." The director is using his strength to get what he wants and beat the competition.

If you can't leverage yourself, you will be at a disadvantage in comparison to those who can play from their strengths. If you don't know what your strengths are, then use some of the things we've just talked about, reflection and self-awareness, to discover them.

WHAT TRANSFERS?

Tennis teaches you good life skills. It teaches you how to make decisions under pressure. It helps you become an independent thinker. It teaches you a great work ethic, how to win like a champion and lose like one.

> - Angel Lopez, president of the San Diego
> division of the U.S. Professional Tennis Association

People often ask me if I ever thought Phil Jackson would make a good coach. No question about it. The ingredients were there even in his playing days. He was always analytical in his assessment of players and the game. He was committed to learning, to teaching, and to acting on his insights. He understood that winning meant giving up something small for yourself so that the team could gain. Finally, he was astute enough to understand that in order to win, you needed a strategy both on the court and off.

> - Senator Bill Bradley in the foreword to
> Phil Jackson's book, *Sacred Hoops*

In 1992, Peter Mesa, the superintendent of schools in Oakland, California, outlined three levels of causes that create social problems:

- *Root causes*, such as poverty, racism, poor health care, inadequate parent education, and lack of opportunity
- *Intermediate causes*, including the need for skills in social competence, problem-solving, autonomy (being able to act independently), and a sense of purpose and future
- *Immediate causes*, such as guns in school.

Court Sense

I believe that the skills you can learn through playing sports can help solve some of the problems created by these issues. Through sports, you can learn skills that will help you become a more responsible person and member of your community. Whether your immediate future lies in sports, business, or a trade, your playing experience gives you the opportunity to grow and develop qualilties that will interest both employers and school admission officers.

Some of these include:

Personal Responsibility Skills
- analytical ability
- ability to perform under pressure
- organization
- self-control
- self-motivation
- ability to make on-the-spot decisions
- ability to follow detailed regulations
- ability to accept criticism and feedback as part of learning
- ability to take risks
- ability to set and achieve goals
- abillity to evaluate yourself
- ability to meet challenges
- ability to make a commitment and stick to it
- ability to accept responsibility for your behavior

Social Responsibility Skills
- ability to accept and work with teammates despite differences
- ability to work with authorities
- ability to understand human behavior
- ability to teach, motivate, and lead others
- ability to work within a system
- ability to respect others
- ability to compete without hatred

Now let me give you some more detailed examples of how various specific skills and characteristics can transfer from the sports world to other areas of life.

Intuition.

Athletes with court sense develop an intuitive feel for what will work. This is something that can serve you well in the business world. Intuition pays off. Often, waiting until you are sure means waiting while your competitor steals the market (or the ball). Intuition means seeing things that others don't. However, it's more than just your gut talking. Your mind is always working, often without your knowing it. The more your mind has to work with, the better the intuition. The more you know about the game, the better your court sense will be. Good insights flow from mastery of a field. Remember when you first learned to drive? You had to think about everything you did. Now, driving is so intuitive to most of us that our real problem is paying enough attention to what we're doing. You know from experience that if you learn as much as you can about something, you can usually trust your intuition when it tells you what to do.

Character.

As someone who has coached a lot of basketball teams, I can honestly say that I would rather work with kids who have average skills and above-average characters, as opposed to the other way around. It's the same in the business world. Businessman Peter Carbonara was quoted in *Reader's Digest* as saying: "You can't build a great company without great people. But how do you know them when you see them? Over the past few years, a number of companies in a wide range of industries—from airlines to steel, computers to hotels—have asked themselves what separates their winners from their losers, good hires from bad, and they all arrived at the same answer: what people know is less important than who they are. Hiring, they believe, is not about finding people with the right experience; it's about finding people with the right mind-set. These companies hire for attitude and train for skill."

Intensity.

Duke defensive back Zaid Abdul-Aleem received a Fulbright Scholarship and hoped to win a Rhodes Scholarship, as well. A graduate student in history, he planned to use his Fulbright Scholarship in

Brazil studying the evolution of Islam and the Brazilian economy. Abdul-Aleem grew up in a tough Chicago neighborhood, but managed to stay away from the temptations of gangs and drugs. He even convinced businesses to sponsor him on study trips to France, Spain, England, and Japan. As Zaid's coach said, "You look at his resume and you say this can't be a college student. He uses his football intensity off the field, too, endeavoring to help other human beings."

Teamwork.

One young basketball player had this insight about teamwork: "I think it helps you when you get a job, like with a team, you have to learn how to get along with people, whether you like them or not, you have to work together to win. And if you have a business or something, you have to work together with someone you may not like or may bother you, but you still have to work together to get the job done."—Maylana Martin, top high school basketball player.

Flexibility.

Being flexible, or able to adapt to change, is a key skill in handling or avoiding failure and disappointment. The one thing you can count on is that change is constant. Every day brings shifts in the economy, the political climate, your relationships with other people. How you adapt to change can be your greatest challenge and greatest opportunity. Flexibility, or the lack of it, makes the difference between failure and success, disappointment and fulfillment. In a study done on family life, one of the main ingredients of happy families was flexibility. They didn't get bent out of shape when things didn't go the way they expected. Instead, like a basketball player adapting to an unexpected move by his opponent, these families adapted to the changes in their lives.

Communication.

I was playing tennis once with a very large, competitive friend of mine. We were in the middle of a long rally when my friend mis-hit a shallow cross-court shot that, luckily for him, fell inbound by about 10 inches. As I walked back to the end line to pick up the ball, I made a comment about the hit. When I turned around to serve, there was my friend, angrily glaring at me. When I asked him what was the matter, he said, "You said I missed it."

"Oh, no," I quickly replied. "I said you 'mis-hit.' The ball was still good."

This is just a silly little example of how important good communication is. As a basketball player, you know if you don't learn how to successfully communicate with your teammates, your team will end up with a lot of turnovers and missed opportunities. You also know that communication is more than just what you say to each other on the court. When you really know your teammates, you can communicate even without words.

Being able to communicate well is one of the most valuable skills you can have. A good marketing or sales person, for example, knows how to read other people. Like a good basketball player, they can tell when a customer lacks confidence or is ready to make a move. By paying attention to the things you do to be a better communicator on the court, you are also learning how to be a better communicator off the court.

Fundamentals.

An article on restaurants started by famous athletes made the point that stardom alone doesn't spell success in the restaurant business. As one restaurant manager pointed out: "Running a place with a celebrity name on it is really no different from running any other restaurant. The fundamentals still apply."

When you learn the fundamentals of basketball, you're also learning how important it is to know the fundamentals of anything.

Mental rehearsal.

Mental rehearsal has a much wider application than merely to athletes. It is sometimes used in the rehabilitation of injured patients. With mental rehearsal, one can stimulate the nervous pathways associated with the use of those certain muscles while they are still weak or incapacitated. Mental rehearsal can also be used to overcome fear or anxiety. Many people have phobias concerning some type of activity.

With mental rehearsal, they can gradually overcome this fear, before having to do the activity itself.

Mental rehearsal helps kids imagine what it would be like to be successful at something. As long as kids cannot imagine, or are not allowed to imagine, being high achievers, doors slam shut on exciting possibilities. A student who can't imagine getting a passing grade in math probably won't even make the attempt. By using the mental rehearsal skills learned in sports, a student will feel more positive about the steps needed to do well in a class, such as paying attention, doing the homework, asking for extra help.

Reading the defense.

The fire chief of Manhattan Beach, California, compared successful firefighting to success in sports: "Successful firefighting is not unlike success in sports; there is a determined goal or outcome of any offensive 'attack,' there is a defense which stands between us and our goal, and there must be a coordinated tactical movement which must read and overcome the defense. In basketball, the goal is to shoot the ball into the center of the hoop. Standing between the offense and the hoop is a variety of defenses. Each run down the court must begin with a read of the defense, followed by a coordinated movement of the offense leading to the shot. Tactics and strategies are formed before the game, and practiced until they are instinctive rather than deliberate. Playing outside around the fringe without any penetration into the defense won't get the job done. You have to penetrate the defense to get a good percentage shot. The firefighter's goal is to get a good shot also—but in this case, it's a shot of water on the heart of the fire. Standing between the firefighter and the goal is a variety of defenses in the shape of walls, doors, hallways, rooms, heat, and smoke. Each run at a fire must begin with a good reading of a new 'defense,' followed by a coordinated attack which allows the hose stream to be successfully shot. The tactics and strategies here must also be predetermined, and if task movements are less than instinctive, the results could be disastrous. An attack from the far perimeters without any penetration will result in a loss of the building."

WHY YOU SHOULD WORRY ABOUT YOUR TRANSITION GAME?

One of the most dramatic examples of how court sense can transition to real life was portrayed in the book *Bat 21*, which later became a movie starring Gene Hackman. *Bat 21* tells the story of an Air Force navigator whose plane was shot down over North Vietnam during the Vietnam War. The plane was equipped with a new and sophisticated navigational system that the North Vietnamese wanted to know more about. As the only survivor of the crash, the navigator spent several days hiding in the jungle, narrowly avoiding capture. He finally made radio contact with the U.S. forces. He knew that the Viet Cong were monitoring the radio, but he had to use it if he was going to get out alive. Finally, the Americans came up with this strategy suggested by an Air Force golfing buddy of the navigator. They decided to use the navigator's knowledge of golf courses throughout the world to direct him to a safe pick-up spot. By reminding the navigator of a certain hole at a specific golf course, they would clue him in to what direction and how far to go. The Vietnamese could hear every word and still not know what the Americans were talking about.

Of course, the navigator's survival depended on more than just remembering the layout of a golf course. It depended on other aspects of court sense, as well—like keeping cool in a pressure situation, knowing and trusting your teammates, being in good physical condition, and making good decisions.

As one coach said, "Basketball is just a game. It only serves as the tool for us to learn the real lessons, the lessons that really make a difference, the lessons that will help us to be successful in our future endeavors."

If you are like many young basketball players, you dream of what it would be like to play in the NBA. Maybe that's the only thing you dream about. In which case, you might be thinking that you don't have to worry about how to transfer your basketball skills to real life, since basketball will be your "career."

The truth is, even for professional basketball players, basketball is a career for only a short time. There is no such thing as job security in the NBA. Look at Patrick Ewing. One day he was the Knicks' top player. The next day he saw the end of his season when he fell hard on his wrist and broke it. That's one reason why an increasing number of NBA players are taking advantage of the league's Summer Internship Program to prepare for life after basketball. Because NBA players spend so much of their time just trying to get into the league, the majority are not prepared to compete in the job market when their basketball careers are finished. In his third year with the internship program, Charlotte free agent Rafael Addison worked with ComCast Cable in New Jersey. "Obviously there are a lot of avenues certain guys in the NBA can take (when they retire) because of their salary. I represent one of the guys who will have to do other things," Addison said.

"This shows you there's life after basketball," says Detroit's Rick Mahorn, who interned at the NBA offices and NBA Entertainment. "This is something for the average player to expand his horizons."

In a *Los Angeles Times* interview with noted black filmmaker John Singleton (the producer of *Boyz 'N the Hood* and other films), Singleton talked about his views regarding college athletics. He was asked if he felt today's student athletes (especially black athletes) are exploited. Singleton replied: "Yes, I think they are...It's good if the athletes can get something out of it, but, normally, that's not the case. For example, when I was in school, there were two [athletes] I know who were dreamers. They were in school. But if they got injured or whatever, they would have been like used goods." Singleton said he respects athletes who can use their physical talents to lead to something else.

That's what is all comes down to—using sports to lead to something else. Some people use sports to make friends. Others use sports to stay fit or have fun. The really, really smart players use sports for all of these reasons and more.

So go ahead and play basketball. It's important for the fun it can bring into your life, and it's important for the things it can teach you. But never lose sight of the fact that it's a game—an *intelligence* game. Play the game right, and you will come out a winner.

AN INTRODUCTION TO SPORTS FOR LIFE

Dear Reader:

For more than 20 years, I have been working to promote the vital contribution that sport has to offer to the education of our youth. As a former athlete, coach, referee, educator, psychologist, and author, I have seen and experienced the positive impact of athletics and have witnessed firsthand its great potential to help build our young people into strong adults and community leaders.

Court Sense represents another step in my commitment to enhancing youth development through sports. My efforts led me to found Sports for Life, a nonprofit organization specifically dedicated to this mission. Sports for Life develops and provides specialized educational programs, resource tools, and leadership training for schools and community-based organizations to adopt. Our programs are geared towards young people and all of the primary adults involved in youth sports (including parents, coaches, game officials, coordinators, and administrators) and seek to enhance the quality of the sports experience for all participants. Working with groups from AYSO and Pop Warner to the Boys & Girls Clubs and YMCA, we've presented more than 200 live workshops (from Marblehead, MA to Molokai) and have impacted nearly 10,000 people to date.

Sports for Life is interested in working with all types of groups on the local level, including grassroots organizations, sports leagues, schools, community leaders, and corporations wanting to invest in our future leaders and make a difference. If you'd like to learn more about Sports for Life's resources and how we can help enhance your youth programming, please contact us at:

Sports for Life
880 Apollo Street, Suite 101
El Segundo, CA 90245
or fax us at (310) 647-6258

Warm regards,
George A. Selleck Ph.D.